India-Poland Relations in the 21st Century:

Vistas for Future Cooperation

India-Poland Relations in the 21st Century:

Vistas for Future Cooperation

Edited by

Vijay Sakhuja

Dinoj K Upadhyay

Patryk Kugiel

Indian Council of World Affairs
Sapru House, New Delhi

PISM | POLSKI INSTYTUT SPRAW MIĘDZYNARODOWYCH
THE POLISH INSTITUTE OF INTERNATIONAL AFFAIRS

Vij Books India Pvt Ltd
New Delhi (India)

Published by

Vij Books India Pvt Ltd
(Publishers, Distributors & Importers)
2/19, Ansari Road
Delhi – 110 002
Phones: 91-11-43596460, 91-11-47340674
Fax: 91-11-47340674
e-mail: vijbooks@rediffmail.com
web : www.vijbooks.com

Contents

Foreword

India's interaction with Europe has always been a matter of great academic interest among scholars. Both share centuries-old ties in trade and culture; their relationship has matured with time and expanded in several areas of mutual interest such as peace, security and both hope to see a multi-polar world.

In this era of globalization and interdependence, there is enormous potential for cooperation between India and Poland. Poland is of growing economic and strategic importance in the Eastern and Central Europe and its economy has registered growth despite the ongoing European economic crisis. It is an important member of the European Union and contributes to international peace and security. Warsaw's contribution to ISAF in Afghanistan is noteworthy. India is an emerging power, and there are multiple reasons for cooperation in political, economic, security, development areas with Poland. History shows that their partnership has always been valuable and mutually beneficial. Both the countries envision an international order for peace and prosperity based on democratic values and ethos.

This volume emerges from a series of academic interactions between the Indian Council of World Affairs (ICWA), New Delhi and the Poland Institute of International Affairs (PISM), Warsaw. It examines several aspects of bilateral relations, ranging from historical, political, security, economic and energy. It is hoped that this book would facilitate better understanding of India and Poland among their peoples and generate wider public interest

Ambassador Rajiv K Bhatia

Director General
Indian Council of World Affairs
New Delhi

Message

MONIKA KAPIL MOHTA
AMBASSADOR OF INDIA
WARSAW

EMBASSY OF INDIA
WARSAW
Phone: (0048 22) 540 00 00/04
Fax: (0048 22) 540 00 01/02
E-Mail: ambassador.office@indembwarsaw.in

सत्यमेव जयते

I am delighted at the Indian Council for World Affairs' initiative to publish a book titled "India-Poland Relations in the 21st Century: Vistas for Future Cooperation". It is significant that the publication is being brought out on the occasion of the 60th anniversary of establishment of diplomatic relations between India and Poland.

India sees Poland as a key partner in Europe. We are aware of Poland's strategic location, its democratic credentials and economic strengths. Our two countries cherish common ideals and values of democracy, freedom and liberty. This makes Poland an ideal partner for India, both bilaterally as well as in cooperation on the global stage.

India and Poland have traditionally enjoyed close and friendly relations. Our partnership has strengthened and attained new dimensions over the last two decades. We attach great importance to our burgeoning ties in all spheres, including high level political contact, vibrant economic engagement, steadfast defence partnership, and deep-rooted cultural, academic and people-to-people ties. Our governments are working together to expand and strengthen this relationship. It is our endeavour to double the bilateral trade and investments by 2015, to strengthen and diversify our defence ties through greater military-to-military cooperation and joint training programmes, to deepen and widen our cultural interface through an extensive dialogue among scholars and scientists, media and artists. We are positively inclined towards building a solid, multifaceted and mutually beneficial relationship between India and Poland based on common ideals and objectives.

I congratulate the Indian Council for World Affairs for this most timely publication. I am sure that this book will serve as a bridge of understanding among the people of our two countries, focus on areas of synergy and convergence, and contribute towards building our shared vision for the future.

Monika Kapil Mohta

*Ambassador of India
to Poland and Lithuania*

The Contributors

Dinoj K. Upadhyay is Research Fellow at Indian Council of World Affairs (ICWA), Sapru House, New Delhi.

Gulshan Sachdeva is Professor at Centre for European Studies, School of International Studies, Jawaharlal Nehru University, New Delhi.

Karina Jędrzejowska is Assistant Professor at the Institute of International Relations, University of Warsaw, Poland.

M. Krzysztof Byrski is an Orientalist, Indologist, doing research in the field of Indian culture and Hinduism.

Patryk Kugiel is an Analyst at the Polish Institute of International Affairs (PISM), Warsaw, Poland.

Piotr Kłodkowski is Ambassador of Poland to India.

Rajendra K. Jain is Professor at Centre for European Studies, School of International Studies, Jawaharlal Nehru University, New Delhi.

Sangeeta Khorana is Fellow at School of Management and Business, Aberystwyth University, the UK.

Srikant Paranjpee is Professor at Department of Defense and Strategic Studies, University of Pune, Pune.

Vijay Sakhuja is Director (Research) at Indian Council of World Affairs (ICWA), Sapru House, New Delhi.

Abbreviation

ASEM	Asia-Europe Meeting
BPO	Business Process Outsourcing
CEECs	Central and East European Countries
CEE	Central and East European
CAGR	Compounded Annual Growth Rate
CII	Confederation of Indian Industries
ECB	European Central Bank
EFSF	European Financial Stability Fund
ESM	European Stability Mechanism
EU	European Union
EUISS	European Union Institute for Security Studies
FICCI	Federation of Indian Chambers and Commerce & Industry
FMCT	Fissile Material Cut-off Treaty
FTA	Free Trade Agreement
GDP	Gross Domestic Product
GCC	Gulf Cooperation Council
ITEC	India's Technical and Economic Cooperation
ICWA	Indian Council of World Affairs

IPCCI	Indo-Polish Chamber of Commerce and Industry
IAEA	International Atomic Energy Agency
IMF	International Monetary Fund
ISAF	International Security Assistance Force
MTCR	Missile Technology Control Regime
MRTP	Monopolies and Restrictive Trade Practices
NAPCC	National Action Plan on Climate Change
NAM	Non Aligned Movement
NRI	Non-Resident Indians
NATO	North Atlantic Treaty Organization
NSG	Nuclear Suppliers Group
OECD	Organization for Economic Cooperation and Development
OMT	Outright Monetary Transactions
PISM	Polish Institute of International Affairs
RBI	Reserve Bank of India
UNCTAD	United Nations Conference on Trade and Development
UNSC	United Nations Security Council

Introduction

As the world is moving fast on the swirling wave of globalization and a new world order is emerging, both India and Poland have been defining their foreign policy priorities. After the end of the Cold War, the pace of globalization has gradually accelerated and the international community has entered into an era of complex interdependence. Free trade, technological innovations and expanding business horizons across the world and movement of people have considerably diluted territorial images of nations. In the changing world order and deepening economic integration, it is often argued that despite immense potential for closer political, strategic and economic cooperation between Poland and India, the bilateral relationship is still neglected. Besides, the current security and political transition in Afghanistan, global economic slowdown, persisting Eurozone crisis, and evolving security dynamics in Asia-Pacific region also pose multiple challenges for India and Poland at the global, regional and national levels. Several regions such as West Asia and North Africa are in a state of flux. Thus, it is important to analyze the prospects for enhancing bilateral cooperation between India and Poland.

India and Poland have a long history of friendly relations. Both countries envision a multi-polar world based on democratic values and ethos, and are committed to the principles of democracy, human rights and freedom. Their economic approaches to development also resemble, and since the early nineties, both countries have gained valuable experience of transition to a market economy. They have close links and a history of positive records in politics, economy, defence, education and science. Poland is the fastest growing economy in the EU and has successfully concluded its Presidency of the Council of EU. On the other hand, India has registered, and is fast emerging as a major regional power. Poland is the sixth largest economy in the EU and India's biggest trading partner in Central and Eastern Europe. With its strong economic fundamentals and good growth prospects, it is a prospective economic partner and investment destination in Asia. Being a new EU Member State with a voice that is being heard better in Brussels, it can also be more attractive for India as an additional gateway to the EU.

India and Poland have traditionally focused their foreign policies on their neighbourhoods and relations with global powers; the level of political, economic and cultural interaction in the past two decades has been average. Further there are issues such as visas for Indian nationals, no direct flights between the two countries, small Indian diaspora in Poland, and limited people-to-people contacts have been important impediments in bilateral relations.

Despite these hurdles, it seems that time has come for widening and strengthening the India-Poland ties. After two decades of internal transformation and strategic reorientation of foreign policies in India and Poland, both countries appear to engage in a serious dialogue for exploring new vistas for cooperation. The 60th anniversary of establishment of diplomatic relations between Poland and India in 2014 is an appropriate moment to discuss the agenda for strengthening the relationship.

There have been a number of academic exchanges between Indian Council of World Affairs (ICWA) and the Polish Institute of International Affairs (PISM) at the bilateral level as well as within the framework of India-EU Forum on Effective Multilateralism. This book aims to provide analysis of the various aspects of bilateral relations and explore new vistas for cooperation.

Thematically, the book is divided in three sections. The first section provides a framework of the bilateral relationship and explores the potentials and problems of a Strategic Partnership between India and Poland. Since bipolar global structure had impacted India-Poland relations during the Cold War, this part examines their relationship through the prism of India-Soviet Union relations during the Cold War era. It provides an account of social and academic interactions between the two civilizations in the ancient times. While discussing political, cultural and people-to-people contacts in details, the section explores new vistas for cooperation between the two countries.

The second section analyses various aspects of economic, trade and energy cooperation between India and Poland. India is one of the emerging economies in Asia and Poland is the largest economy of the CEE region. Poland has registered a positive economic growth even during the European economic crisis and is at the sixth position among the most attractive investment destinations in the world. Although trade and economic relations have been expanding between the two countries, several new areas need to be explored for expanding economic relations.

The third section deals with defense and security cooperation between India and Poland. India is an important export market for Polish arms and defense cooperation offers greater prospects. Poland still enjoys a good reputation as a traditional arms supplier to India, and can be expected to participate in the modernisation and up-grading of the Soviet equipment and supply modern military equipment at competitive prices to the Indian army. Indian partners appreciate the willingness of Polish companies to technology transfer and joint research and development. The section also deals with Poland and India's perspectives on regional challenges such as terrorism, post 2014 Afghanistan, climate change, etc, and argues that these challenges need to be addressed jointly. Last but not the least, the book highlights the glorious history of India-Poland relations and underscores the need for both countries to explore new vistas for cooperation to make their relations more dynamic and robust.

Vijay Sakhuja
Dinoj K Upadhyay
Patryk Kugiel

Chapter 1

Poland and India: Towards a Strategic Partnership, a Subjective Perspective

Piotr Kłodkowski

Introduction

Sixty years in the political and cultural existence of a nation does not always appear to offer sufficient perspective or the well-established *longue durée* to assess dispassionately its multidimensional development, various social or political transformations, and their impact on millions of individual citizens. Nevertheless the 20th century with its glories and horrors is commonly perceived as a separate chapter in the history of mankind; so every attempt to pass a judgment on selected events, however much subjective and emotional it may sound, does have its own value for historians, politicians, writers or general public. It contributes to much better understanding of the background and nuances of history which otherwise is often seen as a set of hardly disputable facts. The relations with another country can also be easily interpreted as a part of the history of a nation as that allows to introspect its own attitudes towards the other, to shed some light on the process of creating images or stereotypes of more or less distant cultures and peoples and to define the areas where the bilateral collaboration would be able to reach its climax. In other words, a carefully designed account of Poland's relations with a chosen country will tell its people not only on the objective spheres of mutual political, economic or cultural interaction but also on more or less subjective and sometimes very emotional vision of the world. India-Poland human touch in the culturally and politically sensitive areas of bilateral collaboration is no less important than the objective spheres of interaction reflected in sheer numbers and facts.

Philosophical Inspirations and Political Freedom

Poland and India officially established their diplomatic relations in 1954 but their cultural bonds should be dated back much earlier. Poland, unlike many other European countries, never ventured to build its colonial or imperial status in Asia or Africa. From 1795 to 1918, it did not exist as a sovereign state so it could not play any role in the Big Game of the 19ᵗʰ century. Poles had quite limited access to many Asian countries under control of the old European superpowers and therefore their imageries of India were to a large extent founded on the available reports on "the grand voyages", mostly produced by the British, Germans or French. What strongly attracted Polish 19ᵗʰ century poets, philosophers, the well-educated members of the intelligentsia and the academic community to "the European discovery of India" was a spiritual message of classical Hinduism and Buddhism. Both countries, due to their political constraints at home and severe limitations on the international arena at that time, probably shared the same view that it was mainly the proper care for cultural expression that could preserve and then develop the true identity of a nation. Other activities, mostly of political nature, were either limited or, if undertaken, led to serious repercussions and counteractions initiated by a hostile government. It comes as no surprise that the metaphysical richness of India became a valuable source of inspiration for Poles who yearned for freedom of their own country and reflected upon the glorious past and spiritual dimensions of the present.

Adam Mickiewicz in his letters discloses a growing interest in Indian culture, which he perceives as very close to the tradition of the Slavonic peoples. He refers to widely popular comparative studies on the similarities of mythological symbols and explains the philosophical link between the concept of Atman / Para-Brahma and Lithuanian Prażimas, who, in its active incarnation, is named "Devas". Mickiewicz's poetic drama "Dziady", considered one of the greatest works of European Romanticism, may partly reflect his extensive studies on Indian classical literary antiquities. He comes up with the idea of the "perfect Indo-Slavonic synthesis" and discovers in a Slavonic peasant, "the Brahmin and Christian, the most splendid".[1] Mickiewicz's passion for Indian civilisation was shared by another one of the "Three Bards" of Polish literature, Juliusz Słowacki. He may have been inspired by the Upanishads, available at that time in various translations, especially by the most revealing formula "tat tvam asi" (*Thou art that*) and by the message of Buddhism. The former inspiration, as Professor Juliusz Kleiner suggests, can be found in Słowacki's poetic prayer "Genesis out of Spirit", while the latter in his poem "King-Spirit".

The true light of spiritual freedom must come from the East – *ex Oriente Lux*, that widely-accepted phrase did not cease to exist by the end of the 19th century when Romanticism lost a part of its literary and spiritual appeal. It retained its popularity in the first decades of the 20th century in several European countries, and Poland was no exception. Wincenty Lutosławski (1863-1954) was probably the first intellectually prepared propagator of yoga in Poland. A philosopher and an expert on Plato's works he studied the treatises of Vivekananda which became the basis of his own philosophical version of yoga, popularized later in Poland. Lutosławski shared his views with Indian readers, publishing articles in magazines including "East and West", "Vedic Magazine" or "Young India".

The list of Polish poets or writers who drew upon Indian literary and philosophical tradition is much longer: Lange, Kasprowicz, Tetmajer, Staff, Sieroszewski, Witkacy and Saliński, to name but a few. Various interpretations of the formulas "Tat tvam asi (*Thou art that*)" or "Aham Brahma asmi" (*I am Brahma*), the teachings of the Vedanta and Buddhism, the literary richness of the Mahabharata and Ramayana, and finally the poetic vision of Tagore in the widely translated "Gitanjali" – all these elements, artistically processed by men of literature, contributed to forming a spiritual image of India, prevalent among the well-read representatives of the Polish intelligentsia. This image was much strengthened at a later time by two prominent Poles who declared India to be their second motherland. These were Wanda Dynowska, known under her Indian name as Umadevi, and Maurycy Frydman, also known as Swami Bharatananda. Both of them were very close to the leaders of the Indian independence struggle and offered their services and hearts to the Dalai Lama. Dynowska and Frydman started in 1944 the Indian-Polish Library (*Biblioteka Polsko-Indyjska*), translating Indian classics (mostly religious and philosophical works) into Polish. Their books were available in Poland in the 1960s and 1970s and the library was at that time probably the most popular source of information on the spiritual dimension of India.

Academia and Literature

A long story of Indo-Polish relations would not be complete without the remarkable contribution of Polish Indology, which deserves its own very high position among the European scholarship centres. The first Sanskrit Chair was founded as early as 1893 at the Jagiellonian University and the Indology Department of the Oriental Institute at the University of Warsaw was established in 1932, and is now the biggest centre for Indian studies in Poland. A very inspiring list of Indological publications had probably a relatively limited resonance due to their scholarly methods of analysis or specific topics dealt with, nonetheless a few of these works (e.g. Professor Schayer's "History of Indian Literature" or Professor Byrski's translation of "Kamasutra") did impress the wide reading audience, who were able to draw their own conclusions, later developed, modified and used in the popular press.[2]

India reciprocates Polish long-lasting dedication to studies on Indology by its growing interest in the Polish language and literature, Poland's role in the EU and its multidimensional foreign policy. Polish is being taught at the most prestigious Indian universities: in the capital, at the Delhi University and in the ancient city of Varanasi, at the Banaras Hindu University. There will be Polish Centres located at the University of Calcutta, being one of the oldest Indian sites of learning and at the Manipal University, rightly referred to as India's top powerhouse of knowledge. Scholars and students alike will focus on political science, economic collaboration and selected elements of respective cultures of both nations. The best pieces of Polish poetry are nowadays available in the Hindi translations: "Otwarty dom" (*Khula ghar*) by Czesław Miłosz, Zbigniew Herbert's "Obszar pamięci" (*Antahkaran ka Ayatan*), Wisława Szymborska's "Może być bez tytułu" (*Koi shirshak nahin*), Adam Zagajewski's "W cudzym pięknie" (*Parayi sundarta mein*), "W środku życia" (*Jivan ke bichombich*) by Tadeusz Różewicz to name only a few. One of the most eminent Hindi-language poets, Ashok Vajpayee, a universal man of letters, has contributed immensely to popularizing Polish literature in India, and that not only by delivering public speeches and lectures on the topic but also by providing the final literary touch of a few Polish anthologies. An excellent sample of his interpretation of Szymborska's masterpiece "Nic dwa razy" (in collaboration with R.Czekalska) is given below:

कुछ भी दो बार नहीं

कुछ भी दो बार नहीं होता
और नहीं होगा कभी इस वजह से
हम बिना हुनर के पैदा हुए
और हम मर जाएँगे बिना ढर्रे पर चले।

दुनिया के स्कूल में हम
सब गूँगे छात्र क्यों न हों
हम कभी दुहराएँगे नहीं
जाड़ों या गर्मियों का स्तर।
कोई दिन अपने को दुहराता नहीं,
दो रातें कहीं नहीं जो एक समान हों,
दो चुम्बन नहीं एक से,
दो निगाहें एक सी नहीं किसी की आँखों में।

****

मुस्कुराते हुए, अधलिपटे,
हम संगति बिठाने की कोशिश करते हैं,
हालाँकि हम एक दूसरे से अलग हैं
साफ़ पानी की दो बूँदों की तरह।

Little Poland in India

Although literature and philosophy do have the power to deepen and strengthen bilateral relations, it is the narrative on the regular or sometimes very unique people-to-people contacts which deeply enriches and meaningfully illustrates India-Poland common history. There are two very unique narratives which somehow epitomize the core human values of Indo-Polish links. The first is on the plight of Polish children at the time of the World War II, who found their shelter and human warmth in India.

Fortunately their history has been properly researched and documented in the book, "Second World War Story: Poles in India 1942–1948", based on archive documents and personal reminiscences". The publication turned out to be one of the most important sources of information for Anuraddha, an Indian director, who made a 2013 documentary "Little Poland in India". This being an Indo-Polish co-production, was publicly screened both in Poland and India. The story itself conveys a symbolic message, which crosses all the political and cultural boundaries. The first group of children, who had been transported from the Soviet Siberia after the Sikorski-Mayski agreement, arrived in Balachadi, near Jamnagar (Gujarat) in July 1942, and since then until 1946 about 1,000 of them lived there.

At the end of 1942 construction began on a new settlement in Valivade, next to the town of Kolhapur. The first group of refugees, mostly children and women, arrived in 1943. In the beginning there was naturally a shortage of teachers, textbooks or the needed equipment but in spite of that all the young people in settlements were required to attend school. Very efficiently the whole educational and cultural infrastructure was completed. In Valivade, for example, there were three Polish kindergartens, four elementary schools, a secondary school, a lyceum and a teachers' training centre. The children and their guardians could also attend Sunday mass, play soccer or organize Christmas carol evenings. Daily activities did not leave much space for reviving traumatic memories. A very special role in the "Indian project" was played by the Maharaja Jam Saheb of Jamnagar, who is still remembered to have said to the orphaned children: *As you have no parents in India I shall become your father.* His material support and emotional involvement in the process of children's education and keeping up their Polish traditions and identity have been pronounced with great force in many letters, memoirs and books.[3] The depth of gratitude to the Maharaja's unparalleled gesture of support for Polish children has been commemorated in various ways in Poland – not only is there a Good Maharaja Square in Warsaw (inaugurated in 2012) but also the very popular and much respected Bednarska High School in Warsaw whose Honorary Patron is Maharaja Jam Saheb, unofficially referred to as "our Polish Maharaja." He was awarded posthumously the Commander's Cross of the Order of Merit by President of the Republic of Poland, Mr. Bronislaw Komorowski, following a campaign led by the Centre for Poland-Asia Studies (CSPA).

The Norblin's Story

Another narrative, which generates very sublime emotions and deliberations on the phenomenon of permeation of universal art into the unique dialogue between diverse cultures is the story of Stefan Norblin and his works in India. He was a well-known artist in Poland before World War II. In fact Norblin earned his fame as a world-renowned portrait painter, having done work for much of the royalty in Europe and the Middle East. When the Nazis invaded Poland in 1939, Stefan and his wife Lena fled, picking their way across Europe until they could make their way to northwest India. Over there Stefan Norblin had already secured a commission by the Maharaja of Jodhpur to paint murals on the walls of the grand palace. He was able to combine both his European creativity and technique with ancient yet vivid Indian tradition. Norblin's interpretation of the "Ramayana" epos, the stories of Shiva and Parvati and his vision of the Jodhpur princely state history have been rendered into the unique language of painting in the form of Art Deco murals. His works should be classified as very remarkable parts of history of art in India as well as in Poland.

By the end of the 1990s almost all the murals were in a terribly bad state and needed very careful and professional restoration. The Polish Ministry of Culture and National Heritage in collaboration with the Ministry of Foreign Affairs initiated a process of the long-awaited restoration works which could officially start after signing an agreement with the Maharaja Gaj Singh II of Jodhpur. Once it was done, all the necessary finances were allocated and a group of the most experienced Art Deco restorers were selected to commence the work. By the end of 2010, the six murals slowly began to regain their past glory and almost at the same time Stefan Norblin, somehow half-forgotten in Poland until then, began to regain his position in the Art Pantheon. In September 2011, the Regional Museum in Stalowa Wola organized the Stefan Norblin exhibition, the first of this kind in Poland. In close cooperation with the Maharaja of Jodhpur and the Ministry of Culture, the Museum was able to display Norblin's works, which were otherwise inaccessible to the Polish art-lovers. The whole event was not only dedicated to the artist, his life and artistic achievements, it was a promotion festival of Indian heritage as well.[4] India was portrayed as a land of the sublime art which combines the elements of its cultural richness with Polish and European vision of universal creativity. That new element was to some extent reflected in the decision made by the Government of Poland to promote officially the selected Norblin-related cultural events during the Polish Presidency of the Council of the EU in 2011.[5] One of the most vivid illustrations of his life and exceptional creativity is a documentary film made by Małgorzata Skiba, a Polish artist living in India who was supported in her work by the Polish Ministry of Foreign Affairs. The premiere took place in the Umaid Bhavan Palace in Jodhpur, and subsequently the film had a great number of screenings in the prestigious venues in India and in Poland.

The Power of Cinematography

Bilateral cultural exchanges and initiatives are on the rise. One of them is the frequent "Focus on Poland" during the successive International Film Festivals in Goa where the traditional Polish Film School is well remembered and very much appreciated. Andrzej Wajda, Krzysztof Kieślowski, Krzysztof Zanussi or Roman Polański will always be highly respected but nowadays we observe a growing interest in the works of Ryszard Bugajski, Jan Jakub Kolski or Leszek Dawid. In 2010, the Bugajski's "General Nil" was acclaimed as one of the best films screened in Goa, and in 2012 Krzysztof Zanussi was honoured with the Life Time Achievement Award. Poland is being discovered as the promised land by the Indian film-makers. In 2004 *Kabhi Khushi Kabhi Gham (Czasami słońce, czasami deszcz)* was screened in the biggest cinema halls in Poland. Mira Nair's "Monsoon Wedding", although not a Bollywood movie itself, had generated earlier a discussion on the Indian film industry in the Polish media; but it was Karan Johar's mega-hit that showed to a local audience the emotional, artistic and commercial potential of the Indian soft-power. The film, with Polish subtitles was available soon on a DVD version and almost immediately found its way to the top 10 best-selling films in the Empik chain of shops located in all the big cities and major towns. In 2006, the top Polish winter spa, Zakopane, became a location for the film *Fanaa* in which the Polish Tatras played the dramatic role of the Indian Himalayas. Both superstars, Aamir Khan and Kajol appeared on Polish TV and probably were slightly amazed after realizing how popular and easily recognizable they were, and that in a country which they had come to for the first time and knew very little about. Cracow and the Małopolska Province are becoming the hot locations for Indian film-producers. In 2011 a great number of scenes of the political thriller "Azaan" were shot in Cracow and at present the Alwernia Studio is cooperating with its Indian partners to make a series of TV commercials, which popularize Poland in the most unusual way.

Apart from literature, common elements of history, academic cooperation, film industry, painting, there are plenty of areas where artists, educators and scholars from both countries are capable of interacting spontaneously and creatively. Drama and theatre, fashion design and classical music, children's education and performance art – there appears to be no limit in recreating the Indo-Polish bonds that are likely to develop in the most unexpected directions.

Business and Human Chemistry

The cultural pillar of India-Poland bilateral cooperation is made of the sturdy stuff but the economic one is getting no less solid with every year. The total amount of Indo-Polish trade in 2000 was US $394 million, reached US $1.05 billion in 2009 and in 2012 rose to almost US $2 billion. One of the major outcomes of the meeting between Polish Prime Minister Donald Tusk and Indian Prime Minister Manmohan Singh in 2010 was that both India and Poland have decided to double the bilateral trade by 2014. The mission was accomplished in 2013 and the optimism expressed by the Polish business community was very well founded. In 2012, in contrast to the global depressing trends, Poland's export to India grew by 27 per cent. Poland is exploring, investing and cooperating with India in a number of sectors like highwall mining, supply of mining machinery, power industry, heavy engineering, renewable energy and waste management, defence industry and food processing. India could look for new opportunities in areas such as textiles, agriculture, food processing, information technology, infrastructure and tourism. People-to-people contacts have always been very good as there is strong human chemistry between the representatives of both the communities, who may come from different cultural and linguistic backgrounds but are able to get along with each other. A few cases exemplify a complex story of successful Indo-Polish business links. The Bella Company, Polish leader on the Middle-Eastern European Market in hygienic and hospital products, has been operating in India for more than five years. They had their production plant completed in Tamil Nadu and their headquarters located in Bangalore.

Young and ambitious Polish-Indian teams have been extremely active in marketing and sales in the South but the time for further domestic and international expansion should take place soon. The growing local demand makes it necessary to consider an option of building another plant in the North. The estimated cost of investment is likely to exceed US $100 million. Another business success story comes with the Can Pack Group (CPG) that has its office in Cracow. The CPG is commonly recognized as the strongest and the most innovative group in the field of packaging in Central and Eastern Europe. They specialize in production of aluminum beverage cans or metal packages for the chemical industry and in 2010 a new line at the factory of Can-Pack India Private Limited was opened in Aurangabad. The line initially had the capacity of 650 million cans annually and it is being prepared to be expanded to one billion cans annually. It is worth noting that the factory was built in record time of 10 months. New plans and projects for the future expansion are being seriously analyzed and their ideas to export the products to Central Asia and the Middle East could happen very soon. Other companies are well-settled in India are: The Geofizyka Toruń (GT), operating worldwide, with a 25-year proven track record in India, is an official contractor for PGNiG, Shell, ExxonMobil, Chevron, Saudi Aramco, Oil India, GSPC, Eni, Total, Marathon and many others. The company is well-known for introducing multicomponent (3C) technology to both Poland and India, and has a leading role in research and practical development of this method. In fact Polish investments in India by the end of 2011 amounted to almost US $200 million and were far greater than the ones in China.[6]

In Poland the presence of the Indian companies is quite visible. BPO Infosys has already shifted its European headquarters from London to Łódź and employs almost 2,000 persons who have a very good command of different European languages, and among them are those who speak Hungarian, Dutch or Finnish. Wipro Technologies, Berger Paints, Escorts, Rishabh Instruments, Ranbaxy, HCL Technologies, Videocon have already set up their bases and/or plants in Poland. In fact it was the Mittal Steel, producing 80 per cent of the country's steel, that opened the gates for other companies to follow. Altogether the global Indian companies have invested more than US$ 2 billion in Poland but the next chapter of the Indian investment story is not complete yet.[7] The biggest ever Indian green field investment in the Wielkopolska Province at Września, has been inaugurated. The Flex Company in its official communique announced: *Our Poland project has started up on schedule. The new state-of-the-art 8.7 meter wide, 500 meters/minute Biaxially Oriented Polyester (BOPET) Film line and a plasma enhanced high-barrier metalliser were commissioned on the 27th of June 2012.* The final project is estimated to exceed US $200 million.[8]

Free Trade Agreement, Defence Cooperation and Global Affairs

Poland and India are able to identify a fast growing number of areas of dynamic interaction but it is undeniable that both Polish and Indian business communities may enter into a serious competition once the FTA has been finalized, which is likely to happen in the next five years. Indian companies will have much easier access to the EU market and Polish companies will probably have stronger presence in India. In Poland, as elsewhere in Europe, the competition may be quite tough in IT and pharmacy sectors. This competition should not only bring remarkable benefits for millions of customers in India and the EU, but also create more opportunities for an innovation-oriented business cooperation, especially in clean coal technology, green technologies, defence sector and food-processing industry where so far mutual potential has not been fully utilized. However, it must be noted that soon after the FTA implementation takes place, a number of companies on both sides may become financially affected, especially those whose labour costs and/or innovation-focused production and planning have not been given a top priority. To succeed in India in the years to come, Polish companies would have to get prepared for more technology transfers and joint ventures with reliable partners who have secured a strong position in the carefully selected parts of the ever-expanding huge domestic market.

The most important component of any bilateral relationship is the area of defence and security cooperation. During the visit of Prime Minister Tusk, Poland reaffirmed its support for a permanent seat for India in an expanded UN Security Council, although it expects India to consider an option of supporting a candidacy from Eastern part of Europe, which is underrepresented in the UNSC. India's defence cooperation with Poland dates back to the 1970s and Poland still remains one of the major arms suppliers to India. A very special role has been played by a State-owned company Bumar, later renamed the Polish Defence Holding, which has developed strong links with its Indian partner Bharat Earth Movers Limited (BEML). For many years the focus of their collaboration has been on armoured recovery vehicles (ARV, known in Poland as a WZT) and the last signed contract to supply 204 ARVs within three years, after a due process of indigenization, attests to a good spirit of military and business partnership. It should be emphasized that the philosophy of collaboration is based on the principles of technology transfers, on-site training in India as well as in Poland, joint implementable projects and personal contacts.

In order to enhance the multidimensional military and defence cooperation in various practical spheres, a political and legal framework is needed. Hence a Memorandum of Understanding on Defence Cooperation was signed between India and Poland in February 2003, and the following year the Joint Defence Working Group was established to facilitate continuous dialogue in different areas of defence cooperation. The Defence Working Group made its last visit to Poland in 2012. There have also been very successful joint-military exercises and more can be expected in the future. One of the best examples of sharing military experience was the joint mountain expedition in India, accomplished in August 2013. The selected units of the Polish Army, together with their Indian counterparts, reached the altitude of seven thousand meters, which by any standards must be reckoned as a real achievement.

Poland and India have undergone the process of social and economic transformation initiated almost at the same time. Both nations share the core values of democracy, of freedom of speech and religion, and respect for cultural diversity. High-level political visits on both sides during the last five years, including by the President of India to Poland in 2009 and of Prime Minister of Poland to India in 2010, are a good examples of India-Poland relations. Poland is fully aware of the political, economic and cultural role that India is expected to play in the world. At present the old rules of the global game, in which the concept of global power should go hand in hand with the concept of global responsibility which in turn is closely linked with the yearnings for good governance and democracy expressed by the citizens of Afghanistan, Belarus, Egypt, Libya or Syria. India and Poland share common experience, *toutes proportions gardées,* in nation-building and practical implementation of economic and social projects under ever-changing circumstances could be inspiring for a number of countries and their societies. It is always worth considering an option to share it actively with those who are genuinely interested and are willing to learn from others' experiences.

A New Challenge and an Opportunity: The Potential of Strategic Partnership

It is also pertinent here to elaborate on the very sensitive issue, which is of great importance both for India, which is becoming a global player to be reckoned with, and for Poland whose political and economic role in the EU is growing substantially. This is the issue of international security, which is related to another issue that is of bilateral political ambitions, which so far have been predominantly regional and centered on neighbouring countries, quite often perceived as "an extended neighbourhood". In case of the EU it should be interpreted as Poland focus on North Africa and post-Soviet states. If the EU and India remain excessively region-focused when it comes to international security, they will be hardly able to persuade others to live up to the international responsibilities that the world-power status implies. In other words: a truly global status will inevitably require a commensurate global security dimension.

As India is looking to widen the strategic space in the changed world and Poland is deeply interested in securing its ties with friendly and reliable partners globally, a rejuvenated principle of mutual collaboration is a must. Both states are capable of formulating a mutually convenient formula of a partnership, be it a strategic or privileged one. The pillars of this potential partnership are very stable and well defined. Shared interests of both countries in the energy sector (coal mining and in a long-term perspective, shale gas), collaboration in a defence industry, no politically controversial bilateral issues, and last but not least, excellent cultural links and growing mutual artistic inspirations are the best assets that need to be seriously considered in the process of redefining and strengthening India-Poland *de facto*, however not *de jure* (formal/official) partnership. The 60th anniversary celebration of diplomatic relations between Poland and India in 2014 appears to be the most auspicious time to finalize it. Both nations can efficiently build more exemplary bridges of partnership which will connect Poland and India for many generations to come.

Endnotes

1   Adam Mickiewicz, *Dzieła (Collected Works)*, pod red. M. Kridla (Ed. by M. Kridl), Warszawa 1929, volume XI, p. 156. Probably the best study on the influence of Indian literary and philosophical tradition on Polish literature, especially the literature of "Young Poland" (Młoda Polska) is by Jan Tuczyński, *Motywy indyjskie w literaturze polskiej (Indian Motifs in Polish Literature)*, PWN, Warszawa 1981. Professor Tuczyński refers to Mickiewicz's inspiration and interest in Indian civilization in the Chapter on Mickiewicz, pp. 63 – 71.

2   I elaborate on the issue of Indian poetic and philosophical inspirations on the works of Polish poets and writers in my article "Story of the Clashing Images of the Country", published in the "Polish Sociological Review", 2 (178) 2012.

For a more detailed analysis see "The Image of India as Created in Poland", pp.312 - 323.

3   See: "The Story…", especially the following chapter: "Polish Refugees and Maharaja Jam Saheb", pp.315-317.

4   The official inauguration of Norblin's exhibition on 2 September 2011 was covered widely by the local media, e.g. the popular, regional edition of the "Gazeta Wyborcza": http://rzeszow.gazeta.pl/rzeszow/1,34962,102 08138, Norblin_i_miasteczko_Indyjskie_juz_w_sobote_w_St_.html; a special press release was prepared by the Stalowa Wola Regional Museum. http://muzeum. stalowawola.pl/2011/38_norblin/robocze/nornlin_info.pdf. The event was broadcast by the Radio Rzeszow and telecast by the channel of the Polish television TVP Kultura.

5   See: "The Story…", esp. "Indian Art Deco – Stefan Norblin", pp.317-319.

6   According to the official sources Polish companies have already invested US $182 million in India (up to 2011) while in China the investment figures are a bit less impressive: only US $127 million. This tendency may, however, be reversed any time in the future. As of 2013, with the support of PAIiIZ, there are 7 major investment projects carried out in Poland and the declared amount to be invested is 120,3 million euro. They are expected to generate over 1100 jobs.

7   Not all the economic reports, both Polish and Indian, provide the same figures on Indian investments in Poland and Polish investments in India. In case of Mittal the issue is even more complicated, as Mittal holds a British passport and Mittal's company is registered in the EU. Therefore all the investments made by Mittal's company are officially NOT classified as Indian. Nevertheless it is a popular perception that it is "India Inc" (of which Mittal is a part) that has made huge investments in steel business and wields global economic power.

8   See the official announcements of the Company published on its website, http://www.flexfilm.com/. The estimated amount of US $200 million would be the result of doubling the present investment. The formal declaration has already been made publicly.

Chapter 2

The Peacock and the Sparrow: Prospects for a Strategic Partnership between India and Poland

Patryk Kugiel

Introduction

The formation of "Strategic Partnerships" has become a fashionable endeavour in world politics in recent times, with India and Poland being no exception. Although the term has no clear-cut definition, it is widely understood to mean the highest levels of bilateral cooperation and special mechanisms for regular consultations on the most important matters. Ideally, two relatively equal or similar actors that share strategic interests would come together to collaborate on important regional and global issues. Not surprisingly, the greatest buzz in India is about a Strategic Partnership with the U.S., one between two largest democracies or between the "Eagle" and the "Peacock" as it is sometimes termed.[1] But what about partners that differs substantially in size, potential and influence and have little understanding of where their interests converge? This situation apparently applies to relations between Poland and India.

Although India's broad granting of "strategic partner" status to 23 countries raised expectations that Poland might join the club, India really sees no reasons to do so. For rising India, Poland is just one of many medium-size countries that bear no special strategic importance and little influence on international issues relevant to India. Are there any attributes Poland has to offer as a valuable and equal partner to India? Are there any strategic interests that both countries really share or in which they could join efforts? Is a "Strategic Partnership" realistic, and more importantly, an attractive idea for both governments? Even though Poland is symbolically attached to an 'eagle', given the sheer differences between it and India, one should ask what kind of partnership is feasible between the 'peacock' and what some may call a 'sparrow-Poland'? This analysis looks closer at the real potential for such a special relationship and proposes some practical steps to make it a reality.

A Difficult Starting Point

Poland, which enjoyed close and warm relations with India during the Cold War and has a huge embassy in the key diplomatic quarter of New Delhi serving as a remnant of the past glory, has lost special significance to India during the last two decades. The new geopolitical conditions after 1989 prompted India to reassert its strong position in Asia and seek recognition for its global aspirations amongst other world powers. On the other hand, Poland took a path of fundamental economic and political transformation and redirected all of its resources from the East to the West in preparation for integration with Western structures, especially NATO and the European Union (EU). The structural changes in the Polish economy and the demise of state-controlled trade undermined economic cooperation between the two. Polish-Indian relations were downgraded and ceased to seriously occupy politicians' time in both New Delhi and Warsaw for the next decade.

The political dialogue became irregular and usually at a low level. Polish Prime Ministers have visited India twice in the last two decades, and the last visit was by Donald Tusk in September 2010; however, no Indian Prime Minister has been to Poland since 1979. Interestingly, more frequent and balanced are official visits by the heads of state; Polish Presidents Lech Wałęsa (1994) and Aleksander Kwaśniewski (1998) visited India, and Indian Presidents Shankar Dayal Sharma (1996) and Pratibha Patil (2009) visited Poland. Polish Foreign Minister Radosław Sikorski's visit to India in July 2011 was the latest attempt to reinvigorate bilateral ties. Even though both sides have concluded a few new agreements, continued engagements between the foreign offices for consultations at the level of deputy ministers for external affairs, and established two joint commissions (on Economic Cooperation in 2008 and on Defence and Military in 2003), they do not consider each other to be an important political partners.

On the economic front, the situation has not been any better. With a strong positive trend only in recent years, trade turnover reached US

$1874 million in 2011, with a significant positive trade balance for India (US $826 million). While Poland was, in 2011, nowhere to be found among India's top 50 trade partners, and only the 13th largest in the EU, India was ranked in 36th place among Poland's export destinations and 27th in terms of imports. Although, India is the fifth largest non-European trade partner for Poland, after China, the US, South Korea and Japan, its share in Poland's trade is minimal, with 0.47 per cent of the total.[2] Mutual direct investments were equally insignificant. Until the end of 2010, Polish stock investments in India amounted to merely US $177 million, and Indian investments in Poland to US $76 million, a tiny fraction of its investments in Europe.[3]

Although relations between Poland and India are friendly and described in warm words in declarations, there is, however, serious misunderstandings beneath the official rhetoric and deep-rooted mistrust. As Poland is part of structures such as NATO and the EU, it was used to looking at India through Western lenses as a strategic challenger in a changing world order rather than as a partner. India perceives Poland as being an element of a privileged but declining global power, the EU. The geographical distance, lack of a significant Indian Diaspora, and modest education programmes in both countries about the other, all make the task of overcoming historically held stereotypes even more difficult. When a majority of Poles think of India in categories of 'elephants' and 'gurus', if not its depressing poverty, most Indians hardly know anything about a country like Poland. The cancellation of direct flights between New Delhi and Warsaw in the early '90s made travel more difficult. A rigorous visa regime, strengthened after Poland joined the EU in 2004, added a further barrier to people-to-people contacts.

Occasional and under-resourced cultural and promotional events in both countries are not satisfactory for overcoming the indifference or for creating new images of Poland and India as modern countries. The Polish Institute of Culture, after many efforts, was opened in New Delhi only in June 2012, and India is supposedly seriously considering opening its own cultural centre in Warsaw in the near future. The Contemporary India Research and Studies programme at Warsaw University in 2009 to enhance mutual understanding and the Cultural Cooperation Programme was established in 2010; but much more needs to be done.

Challenges Ahead

Against this backdrop, new opportunities for reinvigorated relations have emerged in recent years. The current international environment is potentially more conducive to stronger ties between Poland and India than even a decade ago. Now that India's increasingly pragmatic foreign policy has extended its reach around the world, from Southeast Asia to Africa and Latin America, it may be high time to re-engage with its long-neglected partners from Central and Eastern Europe. For Poland, now a member of the EU and NATO, its recent experience holding the presidency of the EU Council has provided the necessary global exposure and better prepared it to engage actively beyond the Euro-Atlantic arena.

Even though Poland's foreign policy will remain mainly Europocentric, as evident in the government's recent strategy,[4] it is now more willing to diversify the direction of its international engagements and play a more active role outside Europe. A Strategic Partnership with China, established in December 2011, is just the most recent example of growing Polish interest in Asia.[5] Soon after this diplomatic success, a similar agreement with India was initiated by the Ministry of Foreign Affairs. As Undersecretary of State Jerzy Pomianowski said at a recent seminar on Poland-India relations, "the state of bilateral relations deserves a special framework in order to take advantage of their entire potential".[6] Although Poland seems ready to engage in special relations with India, to hear similar views in India is still rather an exception.[7]

For India, Poland is just one of many medium-size countries with which relations are not so good as to dedicate special attention to it or so bad to require a strong reaction. Neither the level of economic cooperation nor the intensity of political dialogue suggests these relations should be upgraded to a higher level. An obvious discrepancy in their respective sizes and potential further complicates their relations. It is especially harder for a smaller partner to attract the attention and interest of a larger one, or to engage in joint projects, either economic or political, on equal terms. Poland's population of 38 million, as compared to India's 1.2 billion, is less populated and geographically smaller than many of India's states. While Poland is one of the largest countries in Europe, India, a multi-ethnic and multi-religious federation, is practically a continent unto itself in the South Asia region.

Moreover, there are also serious questions about India's capacity and willingness to engage in any new agreement of this kind. With four career diplomats in the Indian Ministry of External Affairs responsible for Central and Eastern Europe, and only two in the Embassy in Warsaw, India may not be ready yet to get on with new initiatives involving Poland. The 23 Strategic Partnerships already established have imposed an extra burden on the limited and over stretched Indian Foreign Service, making it technically difficult to engage in new summit meetings or sectoral dialogues. Moreover, there is also a growing realisation in Delhi that many of the existing Strategic Partnership documents are just symbolic and incapable of delivering any real benefits. All of that makes India more cautious about forming any new partnerships, especially when it sees no strong or clear reasons to do so.

The harsh reality is that Poland has nothing that India currently wants the most or what drove it to form Strategic Partnerships with so many other countries. Poland is not in a strategic location for India unlike Afghanistan or Vietnam, it does not have the energy resources of Iran or Russia, nuclear fuel like Kazakhstan or Australia, desired technology like Russia or France, advanced defence equipment like Israel. It is neither a global power with a voice in the UN Security Council such as the US, France or Russia, nor an economic powerhouse or potential source of foreign investment such as Germany and Japan. That obviously makes the basis for a Strategic Partnership difficult to establish.

That being the case, there is still good reason to argue that the idea of a Strategic Partnership has not been lost, especially when looked at from an unconventional perspective. Poland and India have similar goals in international relations, such as cheap energy resources, fair climate change regulations, and a more democratic and safer world order, and this makes them natural partners.

Potential for the Future

The attractiveness of India as a strategic partner for many countries is clearly understandable due to its demographics, economy and rising political influence. Although Poland's strongest attributes are less obvious, it has the potential to play a more active role in world affairs in the future. While India is a rising global power, Poland is an emerging regional player in Europe. While one is a leader in South Asia with the potential to be a peace broker in the region, the other is a leading country in Central and Eastern Europe. Poland is a close ally of the US and a credible member of NATO. It has sent one of the largest contingents of troops with the international forces in Afghanistan and Iraq, and its spending on defence is among the largest of all the EU Member States as a share of the national budget. The success of the Polish presidency in the EU Council in the second part of 2011 increased the country's profile within the EU. Although it is still a young EU Member State, Poland has already proved it is willing to play a leading role in European affairs (especially in Neighbourhood policy and European Security and Defence Policy) and capable of blocking EU decisions when it sees them as going against the country's interest i.e., it vetoed EU climate policy.[8]

Although the differences between Poland and India are real, their relevance should not be overestimated. In 2010, the Indian economy in nominal value was four times larger than Poland's (US $1.729 trillion and US $467 billion in nominal dollars, respectively), the same ratio that distances India's economy from that of China's. While India was ranked the 11ᵗʰ largest economy, Poland was 20ᵗʰ. When one includes purchasing power parity, the difference increases significantly, with the Indian economy valued at US $4.069 billion, the third largest in the world, and the Poland at US $724 million, making it 20ᵗʰ.[9] While India's remarkable growth rate in the last decade was on average 8 per cent of GDP, Poland's was above 4 per cent and has been among the best in the developed world, especially during the stormy years of the recent global economic crisis. In fact, Poland was the only country among the EU–28 members to sustain positive growth during the crisis, with 1.7 per cent GDP in 2008 and 4.3 per cent in 2011, proving the stable fundaments of its economic development.

Differences between the two are even smaller when their role in world trade is taken into account. The total value of Poland's imports (US $178 billion in 2010) is slightly more than half that of India's (US $350 billion in 2010), and they are almost on par in annual exports (US $159 billion and US $220 billion, respectively, in 2010[10]). While India was ranked in world trade in 2010 at 13ᵗʰ position in imports and 20ᵗʰ in exports, Poland was 23ʳᵈ and 26ᵗʰ, respectively. Similarly, both countries have attracted in the last decade significant inflow of FDI, and most likely they will remain key destinations in the future. In a 2011 report from *the UNCTAD*, India was ranked third, while Poland was the sixth most attractive destination for FDI.[11] Moreover, when the competitiveness of both economies is examined, India ranks 59th in the latest report by the World Economic Forum, while Poland was well ahead of it, at 41st.[12]

Even a brief look at the 23 countries with which India currently has a Strategic Partnership reveals that many of them have in fact smaller economies, territories or political influences than Poland. In addition, huge differences were not obstacles for Poland to establish strategic relations with the United States and China. If the two largest economies and great powers had no objections to engagement with Poland on strategic terms, why should India?

Finally, apart from the economic and political potential latent in these relations, Poland and India share some historic and cultural links that may help them to put bilateral cooperation on a firm footing. Poland, contrary to many European partners, has never had a colony in distant lands, and on the contrary has itself, as India, suffered from occupation and exploitation at the hands of foreign powers. After World War II, Poland stood with India in support of decolonisation and independent movements and on demands for a nuclear-free world. After the Cold War, Poland and India experienced an economic transformation into a market-oriented economy, even though each took a slightly different approach. Today, Poland and India are pluralistic secular democracies adhering to the same set of rules and values and are fast-growing, emerging economies. All these factors suggest that India-Poland relations have the potential to be much more than a single issue, transactional Strategic Partnership, and could evolve into a comprehensive relationship based on shared values and vision.

Areas for Strategic Cooperation

The factors cited above show that Poland has indeed some important assets as a valuable partner for India. The question is whether it will be ready to use them? If Poland and India are to become strategic partners, they must move beyond symbolic declarations and vague rhetoric and explore ways to participate in joint projects in international affairs. The question one should constantly address is what is impossible now that would be possible if a Strategic Partnership were in place? That could create substance for the agreement. Fortunately, there are some points that can be raised in this context.

First, if a Strategic Partnership is about cooperation for the realisation of shared strategic interests; both governments should be capable of naming a few issues they could possibly work on together in the world. It seems that Poland and India share enough interests at the regional and global levels to give real substance to an eventual Strategic Partnership. The list includes UN reform, India-EU relations, stabilisation of Afghanistan, the fight against international terrorism, and support for democratisation processes.

Poland supports UN reform in general and backs Indian aspirations to play a more significant role in the Security Council.[13] For a medium-size country such as Poland, the preponderance of international law and strong global governance institutions are of utmost importance. Thus, a Security Council that is more representative and effective would better serve Poland's interests. In the words of Minister Sikorski, "the U.N. Security Council should reflect the co-relation of the forces in the world, and India, the most populous democracy in the world, is a natural member of the Security Council".[14] The problem, however, is that this verbal support hasn't yet translated into actions, and UN reform plays only a minor role in the dialogue with India. Moreover, it is desirable from a Polish perspective to secure a joint seat for the EU in the reformed UN body. Even if Poland's political weight is too small to bring changes at the UN level by itself, it can play a more prominent role in reinvigorating discussions on the EU's role in the UN, possibly as a result of post-crisis structural reforms in the EU itself. If the EU could get a permanent seat on the Security Council it would free a place for India, either through expansion of the Council, or the consolidation of separate seats for EU Member States. Thus, a Strategic Partnership with India could make Poland a credible ally in pushing for India's seat in the reformed UNSC, if not at the UN, then at the EU level.

A Strategic Partnership with Poland could add a new dimension and extra strength to EU-India relations. It would be India's fourth such bilateral arrangement with an EU Member State (with the UK, France and Germany) and the first amongst the new Member States. Even though in official Indian rhetoric "Poland's active role in the EU had added a valuable dimension to the bilateral ties"[15], this has not yet brought measurable benefits for both sides. Indian experts would point rather to minimal Polish involvement in shaping EU policy on India and the country's irrelevance to EU-India relations.[16] Although the visit by Polish Minister Sikorski to India in July 2011 was conducted also on behalf of High Representative of the European Union for Foreign Affairs and Security Policy, Catherine Ashton, as Poland was presiding over the EU Council at that time, the overall influence of Poland on India-EU relations was limited, with the postponement of an EU-India summit until after the Polish presidency as one visible proof of it.

The Strategic Partnership between the EU and India, as was correctly observed by an Indian scholar in 2006, "is essentially driven by those Member States which have substantial trade and economic ties with India. It is they who provide the vision, the ideas and the expertise".[17] Apparently, Poland has not been among those countries thus far. It can be expected that Poland should start playing a decisive role in European policy on India, though its voice may at least make EU-India relations more precisely formulated and better heard. A Strategic Partnership with India could give Poland the extra motivation and sense of entitlement to push for stronger EU-India relations and to seek closer cooperation between the EU and India on countering terrorism, stabilisation of Afghanistan and development cooperation in third countries. In some areas, such as climate change, Poland actually shares more in common with India than with its more developed European partners. Also, the EU-India Free Trade Agreement, which has been under negotiations since 2007 and now seems to have hit a roadblock, would bring mutual benefits to Poland and India. Poland has been thus far a rather passive observer of the negotiations, expressing some concerns about trade in agriculture products and inflow of Indian professionals, and was of the opinion that an FTA would eventually benefit more the larger EU economies of Western Europe than the new Member States. With trust rebuilt through a Strategic Partnership, this sentiment can be changed and Poland may more actively push for the conclusion of the FTA.

When it comes to Afghanistan, the lack of cooperation between Poland and India in the last decade was indeed a missed opportunity. While Poland has been the sixth largest contributor to ISAF, India has become the sixth largest bilateral donor of development assistance in the country. More important, both countries share a common interest in a "stable, democratic and prosperous Afghanistan". Even though Poland is going to withdraw its troops from Afghanistan by 2014 along with the other NATO members, it has dedicated enough resources and human lives in the hope that these efforts were not in vain. If Poland decides to continue civilian support for the Afghan state in the future, then India may be an important partner for joint development cooperation projects in the country. For example, both countries may consider developing a joint programme of training for

Afghan administration officials, something they do today individually. Dialogue on the future of Afghanistan could become another important element of a Strategic Partnership between the two countries.

Poland and India share an interest in combating international terrorism. Although Poland has not been a target of terrorist attacks, Polish and Indian citizens were among those killed in New York in 2001, in Madrid in 2004 and London in 2005. Polish soldiers serving in Afghanistan have been attacked by groups taking shelter in a neighbouring country and Polish engineer Piotr Stanczak was brutally executed by Pakistani extremists in FATA in 2009. And as India is facing problems in seeing the masterminds of the attacks on Mumbai in 2008 being brought to the book in Pakistan, Poland also sees no progress in punishing the culprits of the murder of Stanczak. Despite facing the same threats and convergence of interests, Poland and India haven't done much to enhance counter terrorism cooperation. This could be changed after upgrading their bilateral relationship. Both states could improve exchanges of information, step up cooperation between counter terrorism forces and possibly work together in the UN to push for the adoption of the Indian sponsored International Convention against International Terrorism.

India and Poland can more closely cooperate in support for democratic processes in the world. Relations with India are already free of constraints that hamper cooperation with other global powers, such as China and Russia. Poland, a young democracy with fresh experience from its own systemic transformation, and India, the world largest democracy with clear insight into the challenges faced by developing countries, can both do more to share their expertise in this area. Despite India's intrinsic allergy to the term "democracy promotion" and long-held policy of non-interference in other countries internal affairs, it actually supports democratic processes in Afghanistan, Nepal, the Maldives, Myanmar and many Asian and African countries. Poland is engaged in pro-democracy activities in Belarus, Georgia, Ukraine and the North African states that went through the Arab Spring in 2011, and considers democracy support a priority area of its development assistance.

Although the understanding of "democracy support" differs between India and the EU,[18] there is still some place for joint action. More interaction and discussions between politicians, parliamentarians, experts and civil society groups from Poland and India could possibly bridge the gaps and pave the way for launching a pilot project in this field. One area where both could do more together is Afghanistan. Another place in which they could engage in relevant projects is Myanmar that has been undergoing rapid democratisation in the last year. The visit by the Polish Foreign Minister to Myanmar on 9-10 May 2012, revealed that Poland is ready to lend a helping hand to Myanmar's reformists and to share its experience with democratic transition. The visit by a large Indian delegation to Myanmar, headed by Prime Minister Manmohan Singh, at the end of the same month exposed the extent to which India is willing to assist in the reform and development of the country, including through large infrastructure projects, loans and technical assistance.[19] Development cooperation in Myanmar could improve the efficiency of the resources and advantages both countries have and provide cost-effective assistance.

At the same time, Poland and India may explore more opportunities for cooperation within international bodies operating in the democracy arena, such as the Community of Democracies or the UN Democracy Fund, to which both are founding members. The passivity of India, the world's largest democracy, in the Community of Democracies is one of the biggest weaknesses of the forum, and Poland should work with India to find ways for it to engage more strongly.

Second, a Strategic Partnership would give a major boost to bilateral economic cooperation. Although positive trends in this area may continue even without such an arrangement, it would help to create a conducive political atmosphere for economic exchanges, attract the attention of business communities on both sides and send a positive signal about a long-term relationship. The fact that bilateral trade increased by 42 per cent in one year, between 2010 and 2011, shows there is still a large untapped potential for trade and investments. In this context, the target agreed at the latest meeting between Polish Prime Minister Tusk and Indian Prime Minister Manmohan Singh in New Delhi in 2010 to double bilateral trade by 2014 is absolutely achievable and even modest.

Thanks to their long-term presence on the Indian market, Polish companies still have a chance to benefit from cooperation in traditional sectors, such as energy, mining and defence. Moreover, new areas of promising business activity are also emerging. Bearing in mind the rich human capital and low costs of labour, Poland and India could do much more in innovative sectors such as IT, business process outsourcing

(BPO), pharmaceuticals and biotechnology. The success of some Polish companies in India i.e., Bella India, which produces hygienic products, or Obram, a provider of 'Paneer' cheese production lines, and of Indian BPO and IT companies in Poland, Infosys, Zensar, HCL and Wipro offer a good outlook for other similar endeavours in the future.

India is facing severe energy challenges. This is an area where Poland indeed has a lot to offer, from providing good quality coal to Indian power plants, machinery for power generation and mining, to expertise. Moreover, the fact that both India and Poland are coal-based economies and hugely dependent on the import of energy resources gives them common ground for strengthening cooperation in fields such as energy efficiency, renewable energy, green technologies and alternative sources of energy. For example, global Indian companies that have already acquired shale gas fields in the US may be interested in Poland, which is considered to have one of Europe's largest reserves of this fuel. More joint initiatives on gas and oil exploration and mining in India could further strengthen bilateral ties. Poland and India could also come closer on climate-change negotiations, as was expressed by a Polish official: "We could help India within the EU in return for India helping us at the G20."[20]

Defence and security cooperation deserves special attention in India-Poland cooperation. Poland used to be an important source of weaponry for India during the Cold War, but even in the last decade it was ranked the fifth largest exporter of arms to India, according to the Stockholm International Peace Research Institute's data.[21] A recent contract signed between the Polish company Bumar and India's BEML Limited worth US $275 million for the provision of 204 WZT-3 armoured vehicles to India, demonstrates that predictions of the demise of Poland as an arms supplier to India might have been premature. If the defence industries of both countries show more confidence and resolution to engage in joint projects, then research, development and technological cooperation in this sector can still regain an important position. To increase mutual understanding and trust, both countries should intensify their defence dialogue, military exchanges and joint exercises. Recent special forces exercises between Poland and India organised in India in November 2011gave Polish troops a rare opportunity to train in difficult terrain and were a good step towards closer security links.

Last but not the least, Poland is India's largest trading partner in Central Europe, and the sixth largest economy in the EU, may be considered an important investment destination for Indian companies looking for new opportunities in the European market. Poland's relatively large domestic market, skilled and cheaper workforce than in other Western countries, sea access and strategic location makes it an attractive place to do business. According to one Indian businessman in Poland, "Eastern Europe is the West without complications. Technology transfer rules are easier and regulations less complicated".[22] Thus, more Indian companies may seek opportunities to participate in the privatisation of some of Poland's industries (shipyards, automobile, energy, etc.), or to make more greenfield investments in order to expand their operations in Europe. At the same time, the rapid modernisation and development of India offers new prospects for Polish firms, especially in sectors such as energy, agriculture, food processing, sanitation and biomass. As earlier successful projects have proved, establishing joint ventures with Indian partners offers the best chances of prospering in a market that is difficult and still fairly closed.

Roadmap for a Strategic Partnership

Once leaders of both countries recognise the potential for closer cooperation, there will be a number of practical steps that can be taken to reinvigorate ties and give substance to the proposed Strategic Partnership. The first would be to expand and strengthen bilateral dialogue through the regular exchange of high-level visits, additional sectoral dialogue, and intensified Track II diplomacy. Bilateral Poland-India summits held once every two years with the participation of the heads of state or prime ministers could be the main platform for setting the 'directions and aims' for strategic cooperation. An annual consultation mechanism should be upgraded to the ministerial level and would serve to put stated goals into practice and to launch joint initiatives. Existing joint commissions on economic cooperation and defence cooperation may be supplemented with additional working groups to tap potential in specific, pivotal sectors such as energy, green technologies and education. Ad hoc dialogues on important strategic issues (i.e., the future of Afghanistan, UN reform) would be helpful in bridging divides and may pave the way for coordinated actions in these areas.

Consultation between retired diplomats, parliamentarians, academics, experts and other professionals could strengthen the official track. Regular high-level Poland-India roundtable meetings organised at arm's length from the foreign ministries could become a useful platform for free and open discussions on difficult subjects and for finding innovative solutions and proposals for bilateral projects. Symbolic gestures, such as invitations to the country's representatives to be honorary guests for national holidays or annual meetings of ambassadors, are well-tested instruments in both countries' diplomatic toolboxes, and may help raise public awareness and support for stronger ties.

Poland should also engage more actively in forging EU policy on India and use existing EU-India mechanisms of cooperation (such as the EU-Business Forum) to a greater extent. It must make its voice on India clearer and sound as if it wants to be heard in New Delhi. Both countries' close strategic relations with the US give them yet another opportunity to engage more often in trilateral dialogue, and to engage on important issues of shared concern in Afghanistan, Myanmar, green energy, etc.

Economically, Poland is primarily interested in increasing and balancing its trade with India through increased exports and by attracting more Indian investments. This would require more political and financial support from the government to facilitate business expansion in India. The small and medium-size enterprise sector, a major component of the Polish economy, would likely benefit from targeted promotion of exports to India, and special, concessional loans for Indian partners could be offered.

Scarce resources must be streamlined according to selected priority sectors and a few flagship projects. For example, in 2010 both countries "agreed to expand cooperation in the field of clean coal technology",[23] but nothing has really happened in this area since then. In this context, both governments may consider establishing a joint Technology Fund to stimulate joint research and cooperation in innovative areas. Poland should also prepare its business community to take advantage of a possible EU-India Free Trade Agreement through an information campaign and facilitation of business contacts in India.

As regards cultural and social cooperation, there are several options for empowering people-to-people contacts. First, the newly opened Polish Institute in New Delhi and the proposed Indian Culture Centre in Warsaw may evolve into lively hubs and major gateways to experiencing the richness of their cultures. Apart from the standard activities, they should offer an extensive programme of study tours, exchanges and scholarships for artists, journalists and students. Multimedia projects documenting their shared history, e.g. a film about Polish refugees in India during the World War II) could be established as a means of addressing the general public in both nations, and deserve government support. Additional financial resources would, however, be necessary in order to allow cultural cooperation to flourish.

Moreover, a serious attempt to ease visa processing is necessary if both nations are ever to develop closer ties. The constraints of the Schengen zone regulations or the serious risk of illegal immigration should not prevent them from pursuing the potential benefits of more cooperation in sectors such as education, tourism or business. Poland and India are both beneficiaries of free trade and globalisation and should rebuff attempts to increase protectionism while more strongly encouraging the free movement of goods and people. India is already regarded as a great market for outbound tourism, and arrivals to Central and Eastern Europe are expected to increase 65.1 per cent through 2016, from 136,00 in 2011 to 226,000.[24] The Polish government, the Polish Tourism Organisation and tour operators should do their part to ensure that more Indians choose Poland for at least part of their European trips.

Many Polish universities see India as a potential source of new students as the institutions face a decline because of demographics domestically. Poland's government should consider launching a scholarship scheme for Indian nationals in order to support educational cooperation and encourage attempts by Polish universities to recruit students from India. As another possibility to further boost bilateral relations, both governments should encourage their national airlines to consider the resumption of nonstop flights between New Delhi and Warsaw. Even though the current level of bilateral visits (more than 20,000 Poles go to India annually, and around 10,000 Indians make the journey to Poland) may be too little to make this profitable in the short term, the project may still be necessary if Poland wants to become a gateway to Central Europe for India in the longer term.

Conclusion

Poland and India share democratic values and have several converging strategic interests, as well as great untapped potential for economic cooperation. A history of friendly cooperation and a lack of serious disagreements between the nations augur well for strengthened relations. Both are among the top 20 world economies, and are among the political leaders in their respective regions. The success of the economic transformations initiated in the early 1990s, stable economic growth experienced in both countries in recent years, despite the global financial crisis, along with the growing political influence of Poland in the EU on the one hand and India's rise on the world stage on the other may encourage the countries to explore ways to upgrade their bilateral cooperation in the emerging multi-polar world.

Although the prospects for a Strategic Partnership between the two look rather bleak right now, any deep pessimism is also unwarranted. Poland may not have what India needs at the moment, but the fact that both often want the same things in international relations makes them natural partners. If Poland hasn't seemed like an important partner for India so far, it could become one in the future if it decides to develop a more ambitious approach to India. Some kind of upgraded partnership between Poland and India is still possible and would depend on generating sufficient political will in New Delhi and Warsaw. This would require more active India policy in Poland and better recognition of the new Poland in India. One could also argue that with India having 23 strategic partners, having one more in Poland would not make a big difference, except to send a positive signal for the desire for a closer relationship. Upgraded relations with Poland could help India position itself better in Europe and adjust to changes in the new EU after the 2004 enlargement. For Poland, India could become a second pillar of its Asian strategy and an important partner in the multi-polar world. In fact, a Strategic Partnership between Poland and India could bring more cooperation on UN reform, EU-India relations, changes in Asia, counter terrorism, and support for democracies. The enhanced trust that would result from signing a Strategic Partnership would also pave the way for strengthened defence cooperation and economic exchanges, especially in energy, technology and education.

To make a Strategic Partnership a reality, it is necessary, however, to decrease the trust deficit and increase mutual understanding through more regular political contacts and increased multidimensional dialogue between all segments of the societies. Given the fact that no Indian Prime Minister has found the time to travel to Poland since the 1979 visit of Morarji Desai, it is high time to make it happen in order to provide a good platform to upgrade bilateral ties. There is also an important role to be played by experts and think tanks in both states to explore the potential for common initiatives and provide fresh ideas. There is still much preparatory work to be done before both countries can launch a Strategic Partnership, but a closer relationship between the peacock and the sparrow seems to be an effort worth taking.

Endnotes

1   This illustrative comparison was first introduced in a book in 1995: Srinivas M. Chary, *The Eagle and the Peacock: U.S. Foreign Policy Toward India Since Independence* (London: Greenwood Press, 1995).

2   Ministry of Foreign Affairs, "Informator ekonomiczny o krajach świata: Indie" [Economic information about world's countries: Indie], Warsaw, www.msz.gov.pl (Accessed September 12, 2012).

3   National Bank of Poland, "Foreign Direct Investments in Poland: 2010, Annex"; Warsaw, October 2011; National Bank of Poland, "Polish Direct Investment Abroad in 2010, Annex", Warsaw, October 2011.

4   "Polish Foreign Policy Priorities 2012-2016", Warsaw, March 2012, www.msz.gov.pl (Accessed September 10, 2012); The importance of bilateral cooperation with China—Poland's biggest economic partner in Asia—India, Japan and South Korea, amongst others, has been growing, p. 20.

5   Embassy of the People's Republic of China in the Republic of Poland. "China, Poland Establish Strategic Partnership", Beijing, 20 December 2012(Xinhua), http://pl.china-embassy.org/pol/xwdt/t888992.htm (Accessed September 12, 2012).

6   Remarks made during the 3rd Poland-India Roundtable organised by the Polish Institute of International Affairs and the Indian Council of World Affairs in Warsaw on 18 May 2012.

7   A. R. Mukhopadhyay and S. Zukowski, "Poland and India: Bracing for a strategic partnership?", *IDSA Comment*, 27 September 2010.

8   B. Lewis. "Poland Blocks EU Efforts on Carbon Limits", *Reuters*, Brussels, 9 March 2012, http://www.reuters.com/article/2012/03/09/us-eu-environment-idUSBRE8281DV20120309 (Accessed September 12, 2012).

9 "World Economic Outlook Database, April 2012", International Monetary Fund, www.imf.org, (Accessed September 2, 2012).

10 "World Trade Organisation Trade Statistics", http://stat.wto.org/ (Accessed September 2, 2012).

11 *World Investment Report* 2011: Non-Equity Modes of International Production and Development", UNCTAD, (New York and Geneva: United Nations Publications, 2011).

12 "The Global Competitiveness Report 2012-2013" (Geneva World Economic Forum, 2012).

13 Ministry of External Affairs, "Visit of Prime Minister of Poland to India", Press Release, New Delhi, 7 September 2010, http://meaindia.nic.in/mystart. php?id=530216494 (Accessed September 12, 2012)

14 S. Gupta, "Our Priority is to Restart Economic Growth in Europe: Poland's Foreign Minister", *The Hindu*, http://www.thehindu.com/opinion/interview/ article2216863.ece (Accessed September 12, 2012)

15 Ministry of External Affairs, Government of India. "Official visit of Minister of Foreign Affairs of Poland", Press Release, New Delhi, 12 July 2011, http:// meaindia.nic.in/mystart.php?id=530217830 (Accessed September 12, 2012).

16 For details see P. Kugiel (ed.), "India and Poland: Vistas for future partnership", *PISM Report*, Warsaw 2012.

17 R. K. Jain, "India and EU: Parameters and Potential of Strategic Partnership", in R. K. Jain (ed.), *India and the European Union: Building A Strategic Partnership*, (New Delhi: Radiant, 2007), p. 75.

18 P. Kugiel, "The European Union and India: Partners in Democracy Promotion?", *PISM Policy Paper,* No. 25, February 2012.

19 Ministry of External Affairs, Government of India. "Joint Statement by India and Myanmar on the State visit of Prime Minister of India to Myanmar", Bilateral Documents, Nay Pyi Taw, 28 May 2012, http://meaindia.nic.in/ mystart.php?id=530519556 (Accessed September 12, 2012).

20 P. Pal Chaudhuri, "Poland: German Quality, Smaller Tag", *Hindustan Times*, Warsaw, 3 June 2012, http://www.hindustantimes.com/business-news/ WorldEconomy/Poland-German-quality-smaller-tag/Article1-865422.aspx

(Accessed September 12, 2012).

21 With import value at $480 million between 2001 and 2011, Poland was the largest source of Indian imports after Russia, Israel, the UK, and Uzbekistan, The Stockholm International Peace Research Institute, "TIV of arms exports to India", 2001-2011, database search conducted 7 September 2012; http://www.sipri.org/research/armaments/transfers/databases/armstransfers (Accessed September 12, 2012).

22 P. Pal Chaudhuri, "Going to the Poles: Diary of a new Poland", *Hindustan Times*, Warsaw, 5 June 2012, http://www.hindustantimes.com/world-news/Europe/Going-to-the-Poles-Diary-of-a-new-Poland/Article1-866541.aspx (Accessed September 12, 2012).

23 Ministry of External Affairs, Government of India. "Visit of Prime Minister of Poland to India", Press Release, New Delhi, 7 September 2010, http://meaindia.nic.in/mystart.php?id=530216494 (Accessed September 12, 2012).

24 European Tourism in 2011: Trends and Prospects. Quarterly Report Q2/2012, *ETC Market Intelligence Report*, Brussels, July 2012, p.25.

Chapter 3

A Strategic Partnership between India and Poland: Problems and Potential

Rajendra K. Jain

Introduction

The transformation of the geopolitical milieu, foreign policy priorities and perspectives of Central and East European countries (CEECs) in the post-Cold War era have had significant repercussions on Indian foreign policy. The East European revolutions destroyed many impressions and delusions and led to considerable changes in the logic of India-East European relations. Awareness levels of EU enlargement have been "very low" amongst Indian elites and business persons.

This chapter examines the impact of the momentous events of 1989 in Central Europe on Indian foreign policy. The second part discusses the lack of political warmth in Indo-Polish relations and highlights the steadily growing interest of Poland in Asia. The third part examines how the term "Strategic Partnership", which entered the lexicon of international relations in recent years, has sought to be defined. The concluding part assesses the problems and prospects of concluding a Strategic Partnership between India and Poland.

India and Eastern Europe

India was a little slow to make an overall politico-economic assessment of the changing landscape in Eastern Europe and assess implications for itself. Minister of State for External Affairs, K. Natwar Singh, who visited East Germany, Hungary and Poland when these changes occurred, recounts a discussion with Solidarity leader Lech Walesa, who asked: ". . . tell me where was India all these ten years?", a reminder of India's neglect of the region during the Cold War era. The Indian Minister replied: "Mr. Walesa, I want to talk to you about the future, not the past". As a former Ambassador to Poland, Singh admitted: "I knew we had absolutely no contacts in these countries, and frankly, because we did not expect those changes".[1]

Eastward enlargement[2] had erased "the vertical fault lines that divided the European continent for over a half century" and the Union was perceived as emerging as "a politically influential, economically powerful and demographically diverse regional entity in the world".[3] Enlargement offered the opportunity for enhancing trade with a much larger market and a much larger number of countries. However, this posed the challenge of developing a policy that would take into account an ethnically, culturally diverse Union with a more varied kind of economic landscape.[4]

Unlike the past, the Central and East European countries in the post-Cold War era no longer perceived India from Moscow's eyes. The 1990s witnessed radical shifts in their perceptions and assessments of Indian domestic and foreign policy. India could no longer take their political and moral support on various international issues for granted. Much prior to their accession, the CEECs had already realigned their foreign policy priorities with those of the European Union (EU) and its member states. They were less appreciative of or openly critical of India's stand towards the Non-Proliferation Treaty, human rights violations in Kashmir, and policies towards neighbours.[5] Until recently, Indian policy-makers viewed "East Europe" through the Russian prism. Since the traditional *bonhomie* had virtually disappeared, India has to forge closer political ties with new elites[3] in most of the new member states despite a spate of high-level visits in recent years.

India's trade (both exports and imports) from the CEECs declined progressively till the mid-1990s as a result of their transition from centrally planned socialist economies to market-oriented ones, the disruption of old trading arrangements such as annual trade plans, the increasing demand for sophisticated and quality goods and competition from other countries, and their emergence as increasingly competitive markets as they switched to trading in hard currency. There were apprehensions particularly about the *Visegrad* Four (Poland, Hungary, the Czech Republic and Slovakia) would soon be elevated in the EU's hierarchy of trade preferences and reach the apex of the "pyramid of privilege". This would pose a serious challenge and confront fiercer competition and severe adjustment problems in its traditional Western markets.

India is a modest investor in some CEECs. Even prior to enlargement, Indian companies did not perceive Central Europe as a potential gateway to penetrate the EU markets. One exception has been the steel sector, where the UK-based Laxmi Narain Mittal has acquired major steel plants in several East European countries including Poland and the Czech Republic. FDI by the new Accession Countries in India has been very modest. Between 1991 and 2002, FDI approved by India from them was Rs 3742.84 million or US $83.17 million.[6] This is indeed a very low share of total FDI approved into India.

India and Poland

Indian perceptions of Poland in the 1990s were those of "a rival competing for the EU funds, fearing that more foreign investments might go to Poland instead of India."[7] With introduction of trade in hard currency in 1995, there was a contraction of trade. Polish exports declined sharply and Poland had a trade deficit with India. The 2004 enlargement, New Delhi felt, could result in greater economies of scale and increased intra-industry trade, improve financial and banking arrangements and air and sea linkages, and could serve as "a gateway" for goods and services to the vast EU and CIS markets.[8]

There has undeniably been a degree of political coolness in Indo-Polish relations despite lack of irritants. After a long gap, the mid-1990s witnessed exchange of high-level visits–visit of Polish Presidents Lech Walesa in 1994 and Aleksander Kwasniewski in 1998 in India; Polish Prime Minister Doland Tusk visited India in February 2003 after a gap of nearly eighteen years.

There have also been long gaps in visits of Indian leaders to Poland. The visit of President Shankar Dayal Sharma to Poland took place in 1996; but the visit by the next Indian president occurred only in April 2009, after a gap of 13 years. However, by the early 2000s, India began "to treat Poland as a country which was its valuable economic partner in this part of Europe and might become an important ally in the European Union".[9] However, no Indian Prime Minister has visited Poland even after 33 years since the last visit of took place in June 1979 when Prime Minister Morarji Desai visited the country.

Poland and Asia

Since the 1990s, Poland was preoccupied with gaining membership of both the EU (achieved in 2004), accession to NATO (achieved in 1999), and improving relations with the United States. As a result, Poland did not have much interest or time for Asia, including India. Warsaw did not have any "consistent and comprehensive concept or strategy" for achieving the objectives of Polish foreign policy towards the Asia-Pacific region.[10]

It was only in January 2003 that Poland declared its intention to intensify its economic, political and cultural activities in extra-European territories and would mark its presence worldwide in a more consistent way. It was Poland's intent to contribute more significantly to shaping and implementing the EU policy towards other parts of the world.[11] Warsaw declared its intention to become "an increasingly active player" in the field of the emerging European Common Foreign and Security Policy, especially towards the Asia-Pacific.[12] Asian states were regarded as "significant partners" in cooperation covering many fields. China and India were stated to be "newcomers to the club of world powers".[13]

A landmark was the adoption of a *Polish Strategy towards Non-European Developing Countries* in 2004, the first comprehensive document laying down foundations for further co-operation with non-European countries in Africa, Asia and Latin America. The strategy highlighted the positive factors contributing to greater cooperation with India, viz. a very large consumer market, substantial GDP growth rate, developed cooperation with the EU, gradual reduction of import tariffs, inclusion of India in the list of countries which were eligible for Polish government credits, and high intensity of bilateral economic contacts.[14] However, the *Polish Strategy*, apparently written against the background of the mobilization of Indian troops (2001-2002) in the wake of the terrorist attack on the Indian Parliament, concluded the two-page section ("8.2.5 Priority Countries (Republic of India)): "A major threat to the further development of bilateral cooperation is the potential failure of negotiations on the disputed territory of Kashmir and the escalation of the conflict with Pakistan."[15]

Three factors seemed to have prompted the growth of Polish ties with Asian countries: (a) the attainment of EU membership led to Polish involvement in a variety of multilateral dialogue forums (ARF, ASEAN) and enhanced it multilateral involvement in a variety of international organizations; (b) compulsions to improve trade imbalances, deficits and the improvement of foreign policy mechanism and structures led to an expansion of international activity to cover new regions; and (c) greater globalization and interstate interdependencies.[16] Increased trade and stiffer international competition as a result of the "appearance of new powerful international actors", such as China or India has motivated Poland to exert efforts in order "to maintain its relative competitiveness".[17] However, one Polish analyst described China as a "fast-growing Asian market", India was said to be a country with "substantial economic potential".[18] The emerging markets of China and India were likely to witness the "fastest growth".[19]

In 2005, Poland acknowledged that growing rivalry on the global stage posed a strategic challenge and that it was becoming "ever more difficult for them to compete on their own against such powers as the United States, or China or India, both growing in strength" and that only a united Europe could cope with these challenges.[20]

Poland reiterated its intention to develop economic cooperation and political dialogue with the two Asian "supra-regional powers" (China and India).[21] Enhancement of economic links with Asian countries was granted priority in Polish foreign policy in order to attract investments, expand exports and reduce the trade deficit, especially with China.[22]

In the recently published *Polish Foreign Policy Priorities, 2012-2016* (March 2012), Warsaw acknowledged that the position held by emerging economies would "continue to grow stronger". But it was noted that they were not "always willing to comply with human rights standards, employee and welfare rights or principles".[23] With American primacy being called into question, the world was becoming multipolar in which the "assertiveness" of emerging economies was rising. The financial crisis, it noted, did not serve as a catalyst for an overhaul of international institutions to better reflect the current global situation. There was recognition that unless emerging powers had "more say" about the decisions taken by international institutions, they would not be "prepared to assume greater responsibility for the direction in which the world is moving."[24] The importance of the Asia-Pacific region, it points out, was growing in the world. It was therefore essential for Poland "to build a positive image as an important EU Member, capable of affecting its external policy in the countries of the region".[25]

Defining a "Strategic Partnership"

The term "Strategic Partnership" entered the lexicon of international relations since the late 1990s. Though the term has been used in a rather inflationary manner in recent years, there is no clear-cut definition of a Strategic Partnership. From the outset, it has remained a very elusive and elastic concept and lacked specificity; it seems to be a kind of generic sticker applied to enhanced relationships.

Grevi defines Strategic Partnerships as follows:

> Strategic Partnerships are those that both parties regard as essential to achieve their basic goals. This is because the cooperation of strategic partners can lead to win-win games and, conversely, because such partners are those who could inflict most harm to one another were relations to turn sour. . . Strategic Partnerships are therefore important bilateral means to pursue core goals. As such, they may concern pivotal global but also regional actors. What matters is that they deliver. . . [26]

Strategic Partnerships, according to Nadkarni, signify "greater engagement between the parties than mere *ad hoc* bilateral relationships that ensue as a result of normal diplomatic intercourse between states". They comprise several common elements

> ....forging links between countries that are neither allies nor adversaries, but which share a range of both common and divergent interests: (a) they are formalized in multiple written declarations, statements, agreements, and memoranda of understandings that outline clear policy objectives and attempt to build upon and deepen multifaceted ties; (b) they create formal institutional links at various governmental and non-governmental levels, generating multiple interactive channels at the levels of Track I (official) and Track II (people-to-people) diplomacy; (c) they set up a mechanism for summit meetings between top leaders that are held alternately in the capital cities of the two countries, with more frequent meetings at the sub-ministerial and bureaucratic levels where officials explore common interests or concerns, often in joint task forces established to address specific issues; (d) seek to establish a stronger economic

relationship; and finally, (e) they attempt to foster greater awareness of each other's culture through youth exchanges and cultural fairs.[27]

The loose and indiscriminate usage of the term "strategic" has made it difficult to define. It tends to be currently used in international affairs as "a global, long term and comprehensive relationship" between two countries.[28] The Foundation for National Security Research (November 2011) characterized Strategic Partnerships as

> a new pattern of international relationships in which nations enter into freewheeling partnerships with other nations based on complementarity of interests in specific but vital areas.. . . These partnerships are considered strategic in nature because of the importance of the issues involved and the long-term nature of cooperation that is visualised.[29]

Each partnership has a specific character and focuses on certain "core areas" of national interest.[30] Some Strategic Partnerships tend to be "more comprehensive than others, depending on the number of areas in which the two sides can fruitfully and actively engage to mutual benefit and the scope and depth of their relations".[31]

Indo-Polish Strategic Partnership: Problems and Potential

Since there are no bilateral irritants to problems between India and Poland, there do not seem to be bright prospects of upgradation of the relationship to that of a Strategic Partnership.

Problems

Poland is not generally perceived in India as an EU Member State, which is not a political heavyweight and able to play a key role in the formulation of the Union's foreign and security policy. Despite its economic buoyancy, its impact on the world stage is rather minimal. New Delhi has traditionally tended to prioritize in the "Big Three" namely France, Germany and the UK, all of which have substantial economic stakes in India. Thus, when push comes to shove in an increasingly heterogeneous EU, they are the ones which bring the requisite energy to move things forward.

Some Indian stakeholders question the intrinsic advantages or value addition of a separate Strategic Partnership with Poland when its more than decade-old Strategic Partnership with the EU enables it to acquaint

Member States with its worldview, expectations and aspirations, positions, perspectives as well as concerns and priorities.

The meager low levels of bilateral trade (a little more than US $2 billion in 2011), which is clearly below the potential, do not exactly create great incentives for building a Strategic Partnership. At any rate, with the conclusion of a new Agreement on Economic Cooperation in May 2006 and the establishment of a new Joint Commission[32], the institutions and mechanisms are already in place for helping to promote trade and economic cooperation.

Other constraints include a "Strategic Partnership overload"[33] and a "dialogue fatigue" which leads to lack of enthusiasm on the part of Indian policy-makers to get involved in institutionalized dialogues without a political push from above. There are concerns about the likelihood of tangible deliverables, inherent political value, lack of security stakes, etc. Constraints of the Indian Ministry of External Affairs, which is about 900 people, which is half the size of Australia and about the size of Finland. To many, India simply does not have enough resources for bilateralism. While the US embassy in India employs more than 900 people, India's foreign ministry as a whole has less than 900 people and of these only four are working on Central Europe topics. The present cadre strength of the service stands at approximately 600 officers manning around 162 Indian missions and posts abroad and the various posts in the Ministry at home.

There have been long gaps in high-level visits between the two countries. There have also been long gaps in the visits of Polish Prime Ministers to India. After the initial visit of Prime Minister Jozef Cyrankiewicz to India in 1957, it was only sixteen years later that Prime Minister Piotr Jaroszewicz made a visit in January 1973. The next Polish Prime Minister came to India only after three decades in February 2003, when Prime Minister Leszek Miller visited India, followed by Prime Minister Donald Tusk in September 2010. Though several Indian Prime Ministers visited Poland at 12-year intervals (June 1955: Prime Minister Jawaharlal Nehru; October 1967: Prime Minister Indira Gandhi; June 1979: Prime Minister Morarji Desai), but there has been no prime ministerial visit since then, i.e. for 33 years.

Potential

India has a Strategic Partnership with the European Union (since November 2004) and with three of its Member States, France (since 1998), Germany (since 2001) and the UK (since September 2004), all of which are in Western Europe. However, India has none in Central Europe. The only Strategic Partnership that Poland has in Asia is with China and that too was signed in December 2011 and initiated a strategic dialogue at the level of deputy foreign ministers in March 2012.

India could in future contemplate forging a Strategic Partnership with Poland because it is the largest, most populous and the largest economy in the CEEC. It is one of the six largest states in the EU-27 and soon EU-28. It is one of the few rapidly growing European economies which did not suffer from the financial crisis of 2008 and avoided a recession in 2009. Fortunately, it is not part of the Eurozone and the Zloty has insulated it from the Eurozone crisis. Poland has remained India's largest export market and trading partner in Eastern Europe after Russia. As a member of the EU, it can serve as a gateway to both Western and Eastern Europe and act as "a supply base for penetrating markets in the CIS region and the Baltic states".[34] "With its transition to a democratic polity and market economy, high growth over the last decade, its size and strategic location and Poland's deep sense of history and culture," the Ministry of External Affairs asserted, "Poland seems destined to play a key role in the region and in Europe's future."[35]

Conclusion

There is an enormous information deficit between India and Poland and vice versa. There is an imperative need to forge closer people-to-people links between India and Poland. This includes the creation of greater expertise in both countries and enhancement of civil society interaction and dialogues. In order to enhance Poland's brand awareness globally and as part of the Polish cultural offensive in Asia, Warsaw established a Polish Institute in New Delhi in June 2012. India too needs to foster the promotion of greater expertise and networking amongst Polish experts on India, especially contemporary India apart from greater exposure to Indian culture.

Looking to the future, like the EU, the driving force behind Indo-Polish relations for the most part, as in the past and the near future, will continue to be, trade and commerce. In addition to its strategic location in Europe, Poland offers, especially for the IT industry, a cost-effective force, talent pool, political stability, which offers sops for overseas investment in manufacturing and services sectors, which has transformed Poland into a centre for BPO services. The Indian corporate sector also needs to identify and cash in on Polish willingness to share technology.

The idea of a Strategic Partnership between India and Poland, according to some Polish analysts, deserves to be given "serious consideration"[36], but most Indian stakeholders feel that it is still somewhat premature. However, India needs to devote greater political energy and attention to developing closer linkages with the "new" Europe and re-profile mindsets about a changing Poland in a changing European Union as a result of successive eastward enlargements. India does not presently visualize any intrinsic advantages in establishing a Strategic Partnership with Poland, but there is merit in forging a more intense and multi-faceted engagement.

Endnotes

1   M.K. Rasgotra. (ed.). *Rajiv Gandhi's India: A Golden Jubilee Retrospective, Volume 3: Foreign Policy: Ending the Quest for Dominance* (New Delhi: UBS Publishers' Distributors, 1998), p. 154.

2   Rajendra K. Jain. "Eastward Enlargement of the European Union: Issues, Problems and Challenges", in Rajendra K. Jain, ed., *The European Union in a Changing World* (New Delhi, Radiant Publishers, 2002), pp. 46-80; Rajendra K. Jain, "Eastward Enlargement of the European Union: East European Perceptions and Perspectives," *India Quarterly*, 57(1), January-March 2001, pp. 177-198.

3   India, Ministry of External Affairs, "EC Communication titled "An EU-India Strategic Partnership – India's Response," 27 August 2004, http://meainida. nic.in/onmouse/EU-Indian.pdf, paragraph 3 (Accessed March 20, 2006); Statement by PM Singh on the eve of his departure to The Hague, 7 November 2004. www.pmindia.nic.in.

4   Remarks by by Foreign Secretary Shyam Saran at a press conference on Prime

Minister's forthcoming visit to The Hague for the 5th India-EU Summit, 5 November 2004.

5 Rajendra K. Jain, "India and an Enlarging European Union," *Asia-Pacific Journal of EU Studies* (Seoul), 2(2), p. 111; "India and the 'New' Europe," in I.P. Khosla, ed., *India and the New Europe* (New Delhi: Konark Publishers, 2004), pp. 73-86.

6 Michel Caillouet, Keynote address by Ambassador/Head of EC Delegation on "Enlarged EU and India in the WTO Context," at the Confederation of Indian Industry seminar on "EU Enlargement: Implications for India," New Delhi, 9 July 2003, p. 5.

7 Jakub Zajqczkowski, "Evolution of the EU-India Relations at the Beginning of 21ˢᵗ Century. The Polish Perspective," *Yearbook of Polish European Studies*, 10/2006, p. 133.

8 Ministry of External Affairs, Government of India. "India-Poland Bilateral Relations, December 2003".

9 Ibid., pp. 133-134.

10 Jakub, n. 6, p. 131.

11 Address by Polish Minister of Foreign Affairs W. Cimoszewicz on Polish Foreign Policy in the year 2003 in the Sejm, 22 January 2003. See Polish Foreign Ministry website.

12 "Poland's membership in the European Union and its implications to further Polish-Australian cooperation," Address by Polish Foreign Minister Włodzimierza Cimoszewicza at the Australian National University, Canberra, 5 March 2003. National Europe Centre Paper No. 85, p. 4.

13 Canberra, p. 4.

14 Poland, *STRATEGIA RP, w odniesieniu do pozaeuropejskich krajów rozwijających się* (Warsaw, 2004), pp. 22-23. I am grateful to Patryk Kugiel for the English translation.

15 Ibid., p. 23.

16 Katarzyna Kacperczyk, "Factors Stimulating Co-operation with Non-European Developing Countries," *Polish Yearbook of International Affairs,*

2004 (Warsaw, 2005), p. 190.

17 Ibid., pp. 190-191.

18 Kacperczyk, n. 9, p. 195.

19 Ibid., p. 195.

20 Address by Polish Foreign Minister Adam Daniel Rotfeld, at the session of the Sejm, 21 January 2005.

21 Government information on Polish Foreign Policy in 2006, presented at the session of the Sejm on February 15, 2006 by the Minister of Foreign Affairs of the Republic of Poland, Stefan Meller (Extract) 9 March 2006.

22 "Minister's Annual Address 2007: Government information on Polish foreign policy in 2007 presented at the session of the Sejm on May 11, 2007 by the Minister of Foreign Affairs of the Republic of Poland, Anna Fotyga, 15 May 2007."

23 Poland, Ministry of Foreign Affairs, *Polish Foreign Policy Priorities, 2012-2016* (March 2012), p. 4.

24 Ibid., p. 4.

25 Ibid., p. 20.

26 Giovanni Grevi. "Making EU strategic partnerships Effective," *FRIDE Working Paper*, no. 105, December 2010, pp. 2-3, 5.

27 Vidya Nadkarni. *Strategic Partnerships in Asia: Balancing without Alliances* (London: Routledge, 2011), pp. 48-49.

28 Lalit Mansingh. "Indo-US Strategic Partnership: Are we there Yet?", *IPCS Issue Brief* (New Delhi: Institute of Peace and Conflict Studies), no. 39, October 2006, p. 6, fn. 1.

29 Foundation for National Security Research. "India's Strategic Partners: A Comparative Assessment," New Delhi, November 2011, p. 1.

30 These areas include supply of defence equipment and technology, military exercises, cooperation in the field of nuclear energy, trade and investments, diplomatic support on critical issues, cooperation in science and technology, education, agriculture, information and communication technology,

banking, insurance, etc.

31 Foundation for National Security Research. p. 1.

32 The intergovernmental commission on economics, trade, scientific and technological cooperation facilitates cooperation in the relevant fields replaced the one established in 1972 and held its first meeting in New Delhi in May 2008.

33 Since the end of the Cold War, India already has strategic partnerships with nearly two dozen countries/entities.

34 Kamal Nath. Department of Commerce, 19 May 2005.

35 "India-Poland Relations," January 2012, http://mea.gov.in/mystart. php?id=50044513 (Accessed November 29, 2013).

36 Patryk Kugiel. "Poland-India: Potential for a Strategic Partnership," *PISM Strategic File*, no. 21, May 2012.

Chapter 4

Poland and India: Premises of Strategic Partnership Under the EU Umbrella

M. Krzysztof Byrski

Introduction

It is important to analyze the physical parameters of India and Poland in order to understand their relations and premises for the Strategic Partnership. In term of size, India is almost ten times larger than Poland and the population is more than thirty times that of Poland.[1] There is also an enormous gap in the GDP of both the countries.[2] This, of course, does not mean that cooperation between the two is not possible; the doubt is whether the partnership of a dwarf and a giant can be called strategic and will not smack of condescending courtesy on the part of a giant? Nevertheless, Poland should not shy away from it, but it needs solid stilts and consequently great skill to keep pace with India by using them.

After coming out from the shackles of Soviet domination, Poland joined the EU. The EU strengthened the limbs not only of Poland but also of all countries of Europe so much that stilts are not needed any more. Moreover skills to operate in these new circumstances are more important. It should be obvious to anyone that partner status *vis-a-vis* countries like the US, China, India, Brazil and Japan changed radically after Poland's accession to the EU. This has been explicitly acknowledged by Radosław Sikorski, Poland's Minister of Foreign Affairs, in an interview with reference to the US and China.[3] In another interview, the Foreign Minister said, "the most important is to restore to Europe her competitiveness. In China, where from I have just returned, I have become convinced again that we can do it only together – Europe as a whole."[4] No doubt this applies to our relations with India as well.

European and Indian Civilizations: Twins Unlike

India is the most populous democracy in the world, once a subject of the British Empire from where it became independent in the aftermath of World War II. Subsequent weakening of London's grasp of the Subcontinent was very skilfully and uprightly exploited by the charismatic leader of India, Mahatma Gandhi. Consequently sovereign India embarked upon development, initially somewhat hampered because its elites with the towering figure of Jawaharlal Nehru at the helm as the Prime Minister were too much wedded to think in socialist terms about the economy. The fear of economic re-colonisation was so strong that India was fascinated by comparative speed, though partly illusory as it later appeared, development of the Soviet Union. It decided to introduce planned economy based largely upon state controlled heavy industry and strict protection of its internal market. That resulted in prolonged stagnation. It was only in the 1990s, Prime Minister Narasimha Rao, found enough political leverage to free Indian economy from the paralysing shackles of socialist autarchy. There was relaxation in foreign investment conditions and the NRIs[5] began pouring in capital and free market entrepreneurship. The rate of growth of economy practically skyrocketed and till date is quite impressive.[6]

Despite its present difficulties, the EU is one of the strongest markets in the world. In order to recapitulate what has happened so far in bilateral relations of EU and India, let us turn first to the famous bard of the British Empire, Rudyard Kipling. The first four lines of his famous ballad of East and West run as follows:

"Oh, East is East, and West is West, and never the twain shall meet,

Till Earth and Sky stand presently at God's great Judgement Seat;

But there is neither East nor West, Border, nor Breed, nor Birth,

When two strong men stand face to face, tho' they come from the ends of the earth!"[7]

Without undue reticence, it is not to be negated that two strong civilisations, coming from the ends of earth, are meeting daily in the global village that the world has become. The import of this quotation is self-justifying because of what happened on the 1ˢᵗ May 2004. Poland has become member of EU that counts well over half a billion people and to the strongest economy in the world. This makes lines of Rudyard Kipling applicable to the present situation.

It is important to draw conclusions regarding the strategy of future relations between India and Poland, which in the eyes of international law are unquestionably equal partners, notwithstanding the discrepancies in their size and overall potential. As observed during the conversation with External Affairs Minister Salman Khurshid, Europe is in fact treading similar path that of India, not to say following its foot-steps[8].

Indeed it tries to build one economical and in consequence unavoidably political entity out of multi-national population of what is deemed to be a continent without geological justification. If similar criteria are applied, it is notable to see that process has been successfully completed in India long ago. Surprisingly, External Affairs Minister Khurshid said that he has never thought in such terms about India and Europe. It became obvious then that there is an urgent need to formulate more precisely mutual relationship of both these political entities.

Consequently, it is felt that the best way to describe it succinctly is with the help of an oxymoron: the twins-unlike entities. There is hardly any need to make a long list of similarities and differences; it is sufficient to mention few most important ones. From geological point of view, both Europe and India are subcontinents of the Eurasian mega-continent with similar variety of climate, lay of land, population, languages (partly belonging to the same linguistic family) with their dependence on ancient languages such as Greek and Latin in Europe and Sanskrit and Pali in India. Also chequered history of both civilizations, documenting both centripetal and centrifugal tendencies should be referred to. At the same time the difference in the average annual temperature mainly accounts for distinctly different character of both civilisations[9]. Consequently, each one of them created unique system of thought and of values.[10] While India traditionally used to stand for sustainability (or 'sustenance') (Sanskrit: *dharma*), Europe stands for development (Latin: progressio). Since sustainable development is the clarion call of today, this is why Euro-Indian encounter is so fascinating. Europe, more and more worried by unbridled development, tries to contain it in the name of ecology, while India with abandon has embarked upon development at the moment not paying sufficient attention to ecology. History seems to giggle at such change of roles!

Poland as Facilitator of EU-India Dialogue

It appears that the mandatory parameters indicated above should constitute the general framework of Polish strategy so far as relations with India go. Not burdened by the colonial past, Poland should find it easy to accept the obvious fact that it is equal in size of states such as Maharashtra, West Bengal or Tamil Nadu. But India is much more ahead of the EU so far as the degree of internal political integration is concerned and constitutes already one coherent political entity. Therefore, Poland should avail itself of the facilities that are already operative under the EU treaty and band together all these countries. If Poland manages to pool the industrial and on the whole economical potential and market opportunities of several EU countries flanked from the North by Sweden and Finland and from the South by Greece and Bulgaria, the interest of our Indian friends to cooperate with us will be ten times as intensive as it is now.

Certainly this is not an easy task. It will be very demanding for the Polish political elite to take the lead without bossing and without hurting the pride of smaller countries of the region. Here a lesson may be learnt from our Indian friends, since they manage to run their affairs as Indians and not as Marathas, Bengalis and Tamilians! How they manage to find common language among themselves while having different mother-tongues more often than not written in diverse scripts! They got rid of mutual suspicion and replaced it with mutual trust! This precisely is the lesson that our political elite can learn from India. Could we not discern enormous EU's integrating potential that is inherent in our relations with India, provided these relations will be properly assessed and handled without preconceived clichés and with pride but without prejudice?

If it appears to be too difficult to band together at least some EU countries of Eastern Europe region, so that they may acquire proper weight to negotiate deals at New Delhi level; Poland should select one or several Indian states and concentrate its efforts there. In such way Polish presence will be more visible and meaningful. If after careful scrutiny of economic conditions and particular requirements of both sides such decision is taken, then depending on the choice, Polish academic effort should be specially focused on those chosen states, and cultural cooperation should follow with due intensity.[11]

Whatever be the final decision, there have to be identified concrete spheres in which strategic cooperation should be undertaken. The same should be done while dealing with relations in the fields of science and culture. Regarding science or strictly speaking human sciences, it may be suggested to initiate institution of a sort of think-tank focused on the nature and future development perspectives of multi-ethnic political entities. The basic presupposition of such think-tank is a conviction that a meaningful dialogue with India can be carried on only as Europeans, since only European civilisation should be considered an equal partner of Indian civilisation. The Indian civilisation can be properly understood only if Polish evaluations and comparisons refer to entire Europe. As already indicated earlier, this is valid with reference to geography, demography, economy, culture, history, linguistics, philosophy and religion.

It is not an easy task for Europeans who are very much attached to think about themselves as citizens of separate unitary nation-states because citizens bound by special patriotic relationship with their country forged in violent confrontations with their neighbours and not in terms of broader identity embracing entire civilisation. Yet, it is hoped that exchange of thought in these spheres will permit Europeans to see political processes taking place nowadays in both Subcontinents of Eurasia in new light as parallel and mutually concurrent. In both cases, the aim is to make great political entities operative, lasting and efficient in guaranteeing peace and prosperity without hampering internal diversity and without making their citizens less attached to their smaller motherlands. In order to be a native Indian, first one has to be born Bengali, Marathi, Gujarati or Tamilian and in order to be native European, one has to be born Polish, French, German or Italian. From domestic perspective this should be safeguarded by proper relations between the central power and regional powers so that a necessary balance of centrifugal and centripetal tendencies is found. In both cases, it heralds the departure from the idea of unitary nation-state. Europe cannot solve its problems with so many unitary nation-states perennially suspicious of each other and India should never be tempted to create one huge unitary nation-state and should rather be prepared to strengthen even further the tendency to be observed nowadays of shifting main political activity and ambitions of political elite to the respective states rather than expecting that they should have only all-India character and be located in New Delhi exclusively.[12] This of course, should be carried out without losing India's continental political cohesion. In the sphere of external politics, in the case of the EU and India, it is the problem of efficient handling of their relations with great powers such as the US and with powerful neighbours such as Russia and China. Thus, politics emerges as one of the most promising fields of meaningful debate and exchange of experiences.

Supporting Dialogue with Islamic Civilization

Altogether separate and of immense importance is the challenge that the Islamic world poses both to India and Europe. Although considerably different, yet equally important is in this respect particular experience of our two civilisations. Both have the longest, the most intimate and chequered history of interaction with Islam and yet both have practically left the problem in the hands of the US, which has the least experience of dealing with it. Poland should urgently take the initiative of organising the Euro-Indian permanent study group or think-tank on this topic, involving European and Indian Muslims, which can bring in effect foundation of common policy towards the Islamic world not only internally with EU, but also a common policy with India regarding the same problem.

India and the EU separated by the world of Islam should share their vast knowledge in this sphere and should try to perceive the Muslim world as the catalyst of political relations in this part of the world. Neither France, nor the UK or Italy, or for that matter alone will be able to solve this problem globally. This is because of their colonial past, which makes their intentions suspect in the eyes of many Muslims. European Union alone also may not be able to solve it. It is only together with India, that we shall have a chance to achieve breakthrough in our approach to the political challenge that Islamic world poses and propose such measures, which would not boil down to the use of sheer military force.

Poland has unique historical experience so far as the interaction with Islamic world goes. Paradoxically, the past military confrontation in the open battle fields with the Ottoman Empire resulted in mutual respect of Poles and Turks for themselves. Besides the way in which the tiny Polish Muslim Tartar population got integrated in our country without losing its characteristic identity may be considered exemplary.[13] Thus, it should come out with the initiatives to organise such a think-tank consisting of the best experts from both sides, as well as of the most prominent European and Indian Muslims. These experts should meet once or twice a year alternately in Europe and in India and should serve politicians with solid and competent expertise. Professor Rajmohan Gandhi extended a wholehearted support to this idea.[14] Organisation of the first meeting of such think-tank could be entrusted on the Polish side to PISM supported academically by the Faculty of Oriental Studies, Warsaw University and Eurasian Research Centre, Collegium Civitas.

Towards the "Europa International Centre" (EIC) in India

Further integration within the framework of EU will depend on how we manage to reconcile our loyalty towards national cultures with the loyalty towards European civilisation as a whole. India has achieved that with success and Europeans can learn from it. Europeans have a unique chance to be the first to draw attention to this problem. The creation by Poland in India of the 'Europa'[15] International Centre, serving these aims is thereby postulated. This could entail invitation of all willing countries of the EU, but before all those of Central Europe to participate. It has to be stressed that the best strategy for Poland *vis a vis* India is to take the lead in projecting EU as India's 'twin-unlike' entity. Certainly, this will also serve well Polish national interests and it will serve well the cause of strengthening ties and confidence between the EU and India.

The India International Centre should become the strategic partner institution of EIC. Since this is going to be a Polish initiative, the word Europa will not denote our continent but will denote the name of the Greek goddess. In such a case, it would be expedient to invite Greece as the principal partner of the EIC. It would also make cooperation with other countries more congenial for them if it is not run just under the aegis of Poland. Besides the Greek goddess will be a very attractive and popular symbol for Indians whose world of imagination is populated with gods and goddesses. In addition, the bull abducting Europe most naturally will be reminiscent of god Shiva's mount Nandin and certainly the whole idea may become very popular with Indians. Here comes Europa not any more under the garb of a colonial soldier but brought to India by Nandin himself on his back. If we manage to make the ancient gods of Europe and India meet it will be easier for contemporary humans of both civilisations to meet as well. Our mission in India should first of all concentrate on demonstrating the European character of our national culture as well as the European character of national cultures of our European partners. All this should be done with reference to the Indian culture, which constitutes the sum total of very diverse cultures of so many Indian states and it should also be done in the spirit of the dialogue of civilisations and not in the spirit of Huntington's clash of them.

Importance of Cultural Cooperation

Now, it is important to note that interpersonal and the intercultural relations demand reciprocity so far interest of each other's thoughts and cultures is concerned. A good example of it may be an Indian theatre festival in which Poland could participate while staging one of the top plays of any Indian author in Polish translation. The same troupe of actors could also have in its repertoire a Polish play carefully chosen with an eye upon dance, song and colourful costumes that will facilitate perception of it in spite of incomprehensible language.

Further it would be highly advisable to promote with utmost care such figures of the past who have had obvious European dimension and appeal and invite for active participation as partners in the events those European countries with which promoted personages were also connected. Such a figure, is Nicolas Copernicus (1473-1543)[16]. While promoting him, we should invite the partnership of Italy where he studied.[17] In this case it would be advisable to draw attention to the fact that ancient Indian astronomer Aryabhata (V century AD.)[18] was in a way the precursor of heliocentric vision of our universe. Another such figure could be Wit Stwosz.[19] Germany should be invited to promote this artist together with Poland. His artistic achievement could be presented in the context of the Gothic art style, which could entail series of promotion events done together with various European countries.

The same may be done with Renaissance, Baroque and other art styles prevailing all over Europe. Together with Great Britain we could promote Józef (Joseph) Conrad Korzeniowski and together with France Fryderyk Chopin, our great music composer, who was of French origin. Similar names may be multiplied. Yet one more suggestion has to be added. Two great ancient epic poems, which exerted profound influence upon culture of Europe – Iliad and Odyssey should be promoted in India as European counterparts of Mahabharata and Ramayana. In this case once again Greece should be the chief partner of the Polish EIC; entire effort should be directed towards demonstrating the cultural unity of Europe and the place that Poland occupies in its spectrum. The strategic purpose of our promotion activity should be to demonstrate that from the point of view of culture, Europe is a perfect example of unity in diversity – a formula so dear to Indians.

In order to get afloat, the think-tanks mentioned above, the EIC should organise scientific conferences and symposia on Europe and India and the nature and perspectives of multi-ethnic political entities. As mentioned above, the basic presupposition of such meetings is a conviction that a meaningful dialogue with India can be carried on by us only as Europeans, since the European civilisation is the only equal partner of Indian civilisation.

Towards Deeper Understanding

Undoubtedly, both Europeans and Indians have a lot to talk about and they should talk. The fact that India, practically speaking, is the only state outside the Western world apart from Japan, where democratic system is operative bespeaks of it well. It is thus postulated that the suggested conferences could focus their attention upon the topics like the role and importance of natural conditions and their influence upon the shape and character of both civilisations. Geography and climate should be taken note of, the differences defined and the influence upon the particular model of civilisation established. Another topic could be the ethnic diversity of India and Europe. It should consider mobility of population, inter-ethnic relations, and the possibility of supra-ethnic integration while preserving and even strengthening ethnic self-perception. It should be attempted to define how far ethnic self-perception determines national identity in case of Europe and caste identity or the identity of *umma* in case of India. Further, economic exchange should be considered as a supra-ethnic category, which within the two civilisations brings about integration of separate communities. This aspect of development of both civilisations should be investigated in historical perspective. Also, the degree in which economic exchange participates in bringing about the awareness of belonging to one civilisation should be determined. It would be useful to define the role of this aspect in current political processes happening in both Subcontinents.

A question arises here; should history be perceived exclusively as a register of irreconcilable differences, of conflicts not to be solved and mistrusts not to be eliminated and as a chronicle of short-sightedness and misunderstandings? Should it be rather understood as a process of growing 'civilisational' awareness? As already indicated, separate and minute attention should be given to the investigation of Euro-Islamic and Indo-Islamic history, which should be carefully compared. On the whole, the exchange of analyses and evaluations made on a 'sub continental' scale in both cases can help to strengthen pro-integration tendencies among Europeans and Indians as well.

Problem of multi-lingual character of Europe and India and the need to build the thesaurus of common vocabulary is also an issue worth tackling. The linguistic situation of both entities should be described and defined. An effort to pinpoint the hazards of integration processes on one hand and of preserving proper identity of different languages on the other, should be undertaken. These deliberations could provide necessary expertise for the parliaments of Europe and India regarding the actual 'sub continental' linguistic policy. The integration potential inherent in the classical languages of both civilisations should be taken note of.

Last but not the least, the role of common value system in the integration process of civilisation-states (in contradiction to nation-states) should be considered. The basic elements of these systems should be identified and their integration potential analysed. So far as the semantic content of terminology is concerned, suitable source material can be found in philosophy, religion and philology. We have in mind here such terms among others as Indian *dharma* and European ethics. The purpose of dealing with these topics is to answer among others a question; what lies behind the process of political unification of large communities, the integrating factor of which is civilisation? Yet another question that may be answered is whether the feedback relationship, which takes place between technology and quality of human existence, strengthens or weakens this process? Here interaction between science and technology representatives should be brought about and Polish scientists enjoying universal acclaim and having successful careers in various European countries could play an important role.

Besides these problems, religions should also be considered within the purview of the activities of EIC. The dialogue of representatives of Christianity, Islam, Hinduism and Buddhism, though elitist in nature, might have a broader impact which should never be undervalued. The problem of Islam has already been touched upon earlier as the most crucial for both Europe and India. But also the meeting of Christianity with Hinduism and Buddhism in an unprejudiced debate may become very fruitful in bringing both civilisations closer to each other. We are convinced that these religions are not as far apart as they generally are deemed to be.

There is no dearth of institutions in India, which may be looked up to for cooperation and invited as partners of centre. Just to exemplify, it can be mentioned besides India International Centre, such establishments like the Indian Council for Cultural Relations, Institute for the Study of Developing Societies, Institute for Defence Studies and Analyses, Sangit Natak Akademi, Sahitya Akademi, Lalit Kala Akademi all located in Delhi. Outside Delhi it could be *Bharat Bhavan* in Bhopal and *Kalidasa Akademi* in Madhya Pradesh and *Kalamandalam* w Cheruthuruthy in Kerala, etc

To conclude, it can be stated that the basic premise for such understanding of strategic partnership between Europeans and Indians, initiated and promoted by Poland is in the sphere of politics, economy, defense and culture. It is a conviction that structural parallels between European and Indian civilisations exist. Moreover, both civilisations confront similar challenges.

Endnotes

1 According to *Encyclopaedia Britannica population of Poland* (2011 est.) is 38,216,000 and *total area (sq mi) is* 120,726 *and (sq km) is* 312,679, while *population of India* (2011 est.) is 1,216,728,000 and *total area (sq mi) is* 1,222,559 *and area (sq km) is* 3,166,414.

2 The GDP of India with regards to purchasing power parity is approximately 4.463 trillion dollars, which places it in the 4th position in the world. With regards to official exchange rate its GDP is close to $1.843 trillion. http://business.mapsofindia.com/india-gdp /(Accessed September 19, 2012). The GDP of Poland is US $ 528.46 billion (2011 estimate) http://www.gfmag.com/gdp-data-country-reports/197-poland-gdp-country-report.html#axzz26ueIGu7X (Accessed September 19, 2012).

3 TVN TV station broadcasted this interview by Monika Olejnik in her *'Kropka nad i'* programme on the 19 September 2012.

4 Gazeta Wyborcza, 19 September 2012, p. 4.

5 "An Indian Citizen who stays abroad for employment/carrying on business or vocation outside India or stays abroad under circumstances indicating an intention for an uncertain duration of stay abroad is a non-resident. (Persons posted in U.N. Organisations and Officials deputed abroad by Central/State Governments and Public Sector undertakings on temporary assignments are also treated as non-residents). Non –Resident foreign citizens of Indian Origin are treated on par with non-resident Indian Citizens (NRIs) for the purpose of certain facilities." http://www.vakilno1.com/nri/taxation/definitions.htm (Accessed September 23, 2012).

6 "The Gross Domestic Product (GDP) in India expanded 0.8 percent in the second quarter of 2012 over the previous quarter. Historically, from 1996 until 2012, India GDP Growth Rate averaged 1.65 Percent reaching an all time high of 6.10 Percent in March of 2010 and a record low of -1.50 Percent in March of 2004. The Gross Domestic Product (GDP) growth rate provides an aggregated measure of changes in value of the goods and services produced by an economy.....The economy has posted an average growth rate of more than 7% in the decade since 1997, reducing poverty by about 10 percentage points." http://www.tradingeconomics.com/india/gdp-growth (Accessed date: 20 September 2012).

7 *The Ballad of East and West* in *Barrack Room Ballads Departmental Ditties,* by Rudyard Kipling (New York: Arcadia House, 1950), pp. 137-144.

8 The author's interview with Minister Salman Khurshid. He was Union Minister of State, External Affairs January 1993 until June 1996.

9 Nirad Chaudhuri attaches great importance to temperature as a factor determining the character of civilisations. (See his *passage to England,* The Hogarth Press Ltd; New edition (November 1989).

10 Both geographical units are subcontinents of Asia. The European north-western Subcontinent of 10 529 000 square kilometres (4 882 000 kilometres without the erstwhile Soviet Union) and the Indian southern Subcontinent of 5 479 998 square kilometres. While India is a compact landmass, Europe is a sort of peninsula interspersed with huge stretches of inland [Mediterranean] seas. The quoted *Encyclopaedia* enumerates 27 such seas. The character of the lie of the land in both cases is equally varied though this variety is distributed differently. Climate again in both cases is equally varied but the average annual temperature differs immensely. In India the maximal one is +26, 8 C and minimal is +18.10 C. The European one in turn is +17.11 C and — 8.08

C. The important difference is that in most of Europe - for well over half a year – the climate is lethal for an unclad man. Populations wise both similarity and difference is hidden in number. In Indian Subcontinent by the beginning of this century the total was around 1 412 100 000 [2002] and in Europe without the Soviet part of it, it was around 513 000 000 [1994].(See *Encyklopedia Geograficzna Świata – Europa,* Opress, Kraków 1996.)

11 This thought was originally presented by Professor Shrikant Paranjape, Department of Defense and Strategic Studies, University of Pune during the debate at the 3rd PISM-ICWA Roundtable Conference in Warsaw on the 17th of May 2012.

12 Also see Byrski, M.K., The Indian *Jāti* and the European *Nation*; The Twins-Unlike Concepts of Mega-Tribal Level, in *Polish Sociological Research Review,* 2 (178), 2012, pp.167-185.

13 Tartars amounting to 447 citizens of Poland, live in indigenous Tartar colonies in Podlaskie Voivodship (Bohoniki and Kruszyniany) (319), Pomorskie Voivodship (28), Mazowieckie Voivodship (22), Wielkopolskie Voivodship– (20). Until the end of the 14th century, Polish Tartars used to live in the lands of the Grand Lithuanian Duchy. Their predecessors were either émigrés or refugees from the Golden Horde or Crimea. The mother tongue of the Polish Tartars has become extinct and they have no schools of their own. http://www.msw.gov.pl/palm/en/10/56/Characteristics_ of_ethnic_and_national_minorities_in_Poland.html (Accessed 23 September 2012). See also: Anna Cieslik and Maykel Verkuyten, *National, Ethnic and Religious Identities: Hybridity and the case of the Polish Tatars,* in 'National Identities', Vol. 8, No. 2, June 2006, pp. 77-93.

14 "He has worked consistently for India-Pakistan and Hindu-Muslim reconciliation. Since 9/11, he has also tried to address the divide between the West and the world of Islam." http://www.dbqdayofpeace.org/rajmohan-gandhi-biography.html (Accessed September 23,2012). Rajmohan Gandhi among other authored a book entitled *Understanding the Muslim Mind,* (Kolkata: Penguin Books, 1990).

15 The Greek goddess *'ΕΥΡΩΠΗ'* is meant here, who is pictured as sitting on the back of a bull after he abducted her (*Europaharanam* in the Sanskrit language) and which may be taken for the famous Nandi, the riding of god Shiva – an association, which may have a mighty promotion value in India.

16 There is an avenue in New Delhi bearing his name.

17 See Wolfram Research, http://scienceworld.wolfram.com/biography/Copernicus.html.

18 See Takao Hayashi's entry in http://www.britannica.com/EBchecked/topic/37461/Aryabhata-I.

19 Veit Stoss in German. He was "born in 1438/47, in Swabia and died in 1533, in Nuremberg. He was a German sculptor and wood carver. He worked mainly in Poland from 1477 to 1496." http://www.answers.com/topic/veit-stoss. (Accessed September 25, 2012).

Chapter 5

India-Poland Economic Relations in the Context of broader India-EU Ties and Euro Crisis

Gulshan Sachdeva

Introduction

Even under a centrally planned economy, the Polish socialist project used to be one of the most innovative in Central and Eastern Europe (CEE). Therefore, despite initial disequilibrium, Poland entered the post-socialist era with a relatively favourable position. Transformation from a centrally planned economy to a market economy was a complex process, which involved institutional, structural as well as behavioral changes. Therefore, even under the best of circumstances, it entailed large difficulties and transition cost. As a result, all CEE countries including Poland faced serious challenges in the initial stages of their economic transformation. Most of these countries entered into the process of transition with large monetary overhangs and repressed inflation. Since there was hardly any precedence of an economy moving directly from a centrally planned system to a market economy, there was no single blueprint for reforms available to these countries. The theoretical knowledge of this emerging new branch of economics was also insufficient. As a result, the focus in the initial few years was on economic policy issues of stabilization, liberalization and privatization, and their sequencing and speed.

Based on the Polish approach, few basic guidelines were considered necessary for transformation towards a market system. The first and the most important guideline was that if the economy was in a serious state of disequilibrium, then stabilization should be given first priority. Despite little variations, it was understood that macroeconomic stabilization meant bringing repressed and/or open inflation under control, through restrictive monetary measures and reduction in unsustainable budget deficits. This also entailed the removal of price controls and reduction in subsidies to discipline economic agents (both firms and consumers). Under liberalization, it was understood in the region that the economy should be open to international trade and factor movements. This would include reducing import and export restrictions, liberal rules for foreign investment, implementation of uniform exchange rates if they were not in place, conversion of quotas to tariffs etc. If it is possible, some form of convertibility was also recommended to link domestic enterprises with the world economy. In the institutional structural side, the establishment of private property rights and divestiture of state property was also considered necessary. Emphasis was also given on creating market institutions like competition, financial intermediaries and new tax systems etc. Generally a "social safety net" was also recommended for those who might suffer from short term costs of transformation.

The next important question was on the sequencing of these reforms. Another interrelated and important issue was the appropriate speed of the implementation of transformation, in other words, whether the transformation requires `shock therapy' or a 'gradual' approach. Polish policy makers clearly chose the big-bang approach. After initial debates, however, it was more or less settled that rapid policy action was possible in some areas of reform - price and trade liberalization, initial inflation stabilization and possibly small-scale privatization. However, in other areas it was realized that it would take longer time. Later, it was asserted by the World Bank in its studies that although liberalization, stabilization and privatization were intrinsic to transition, they were not enough to create vibrant market economies. It was argued that building on the early gains of transition will require major consolidating reforms, strong market supporting institutions, a skilled and adaptable work force and full integration into the world economy

On the basis of these guidelines, Poland has successfully undertaken economic and political transition from a centrally planned economy to a market economy. The country has already established fundamental institutions of democracy and market economy which will allow the country to witness sustained economic growth in the medium run. The country became member of the EU in 2004 and has also been successfully integrated into organizations like the WTO, OECD and NATO. Poland also provided one of the most positive environments for foreign investors among EU's new Member States. The Polish economic transformation to a market economy in the early 1990s coincided with the Indian economic reforms aimed at liberalizing highly controlled mixed market economy. Since 1992, India is also making a successful transition from an excessively inward-oriented economy to a more globally integrated economy. As a result of new policies, it has become one of the fastest growing economies of the world. Despite some serious challenges, like energy security, poverty, infrastructure, regional disparities and internal security, there are strong indications that rapid growth will continue. In the present situation, when Poland is an integral part of the EU, any major policy initiative affecting bilateral ties has to be consistent with the broader India-EU relations. Similarly, when the European economy in general and the Eurozone is facing a serious economic and financial crisis in the last three years, India-Poland economic relations are bound to be affected by these broader economic trends. In this paper, an attempt has been made to look into India-Poland economic relations within these broader trends.

India's Economic Relations with the CEE

Links between India and some of the CEE countries including Poland date back in time and there are traces of contacts among these countries as early as the 8th century A.D. In the medieval ages, the Kingdom of Bohemia (now in the Czech Republic) traded with India. Indian culture enjoys considerable popularity in some of these countries. India's relations with all CEE countries are deep rooted and have traditionally been close and friendly. There are no fundamental disagreements on important political issues between India and any of the country in the CEE region. There has been close cooperation between India and the CEE countries in various international forums.

During the Soviet period, the nature and character of the then Indo-Soviet relations broadly determined economic relations between India and CEE countries. These relations were institutionalized through Rupee-Rouble trade agreements with most individual countries. The relations operated through the negotiations of annual protocols which fixed the products to be traded and amounts thereof, with the trade being channelized through government agencies. In the later periods, hard currency trade terms were introduced to replace rupee trade/barter system with some of these countries.

In the post-socialist era, trade and economic relations between India and the CEE region declined considerably. One of the major causes was the economic decline in the region following stabilization and liberalization policies in the region in the early nineties. More important reason was however, changing orientation of CEE firms towards western European markets. Because of trade liberalization in the region, Indian companies had to compete with well-established neighbouring European companies. From the early 1990s itself, the Indian government encouraged bilateral economic relations with all CEE countries.

Although in the 1990's these countries created many opportunities due to their liberal economic policy regimes, Indian companies were not able to take much advantage. One major reason was that traditional actors like public sector units and state trading companies, through which Indian companies interacted earlier in the region, vanished quickly. Private initiatives to fill this gap have been slow. This has been mainly due to Euro-centric approach of CEE countries and less aggressive nature of most Indian companies. Despite having excellent socio-political relations in the past, no policy action towards improving trade and economic relations was taken in the 1990's because of Euro centracism of CEE countries and lack of imaginative policy framework for transition economies by Indian policy makers. As a result, India's economic presence in the region declined substantially. Since 2004 when most of these countries became part of the EU, the whole region, particularly big markets like Poland, are difficult to neglect. Geographically situated adjacent to large dynamic markets and enjoying special trade privileges with those countries, CEE is well positioned and has considerable commercial potential. In the last fifteen years, growth rates in many countries of the region have been one of the highest in the world. Since most of the countries from the CEE group have become members of the EU, bilateral economic relations with these countries have to be seen within the broader India-EU economic ties.

India-EU Economic Ties

In the last two decades, India's global vision of a democratic, multicultural and multipolar world coincides with that of Europe. Similarly, while a new economic and security architecture is evolving in Asia, Europe's engagement with Asia will be incomplete unless it partners India. Realizing the importance of this, the two entities instituted annual summit meetings (supplemented by business summits) in 2000. These meetings resulted in the India-EU Strategic Partnership (2004) and launched a Joint Action Plan in 2005 at the sixth summit in Delhi. In 2006, India was invited to join the Asia-Europe Meeting (ASEM), an informal process of dialogue between Asia and Europe.

Historically, trade and economic relations with Europe have always been important for India and formed the core of India-European Economic Community (EEC)/EU relations. At the very first annual summit (2000), India and the EU agreed to enhance trade and cooperation. The 11th EU Joint Commission encouraged industry to launch the Joint Initiative to Enhance Trade and Investment. Twelve summits have so far taken place with the last one in Delhi in February 2012. The agenda for these summits has been set by the prevailing economic, political and strategic environment. Major issues discussed during the last few summits include trade and economic issues, energy and climate change, the global economic situation and governance, and global and regional security issues, particularly Afghanistan.[1]

In recent years, Indian exports to the EU-27 have increased from about US$ 8.8 billion in 1996-97 to about US$ 53 billion in 2011-12.[2] Similarly, India imported commodities worth US$ 58 billion in the same year from the EU. This was nearly a six-fold increase from imports of US$ 10.6 billion in 1996-97. Due to the global economic slowdown, bilateral trade declined to about US$74 billion in 2009-10, with US$36 billion in exports and US$38 billion in imports. Bilateral trade, however, has recovered again in the last two years. India's major trading partners in the EU-27 are Germany, Belgium, the UK, the Netherlands, Italy and France. In 2011-12, these six countries accounted for about 80 per cent of India's trade with the Union. The remaining 21 countries accounted for only 20 per cent of total trade with the EU-27. In recent years, imports from Sweden have witnessed a major spurt. For many years, the UK has been the major export market within the EU, accounting for 19 per cent of exports to the EU 27 and about 4 per cent of total Indian exports in 2007–08. In recent years, however, the Netherlands has become India's biggest export market within the EU.

Services are becoming increasingly important in India-EU trade. In fact, issues concerning services will determine fate of bilateral negotiations on the Broad-Based Bilateral Trade and Investment Agreement. In 2008, the share of services (including construction) in the EU gross value added was 78.1 per cent. In the same year, services accounted for about 55 per cent of the Indian economy. The EU is the biggest global player in the international trade in services. In 2008, the EU's international trade in services recorded a surplus of €75.4 billion. Its total trade in services was €965 billion (€520 billion exports and €445 billion imports). India is also becoming a significant player in the global services trade. India's trade in services with the EU-27 grew from €7.8 billion in 2004 to about €17.9 billion in 2010. In recent years, India has recorded a surplus in travel, computer and information and communication services. The total deficit recorded with the EU was about €1.4 billion in 2008 and €1.7 billion in 2010. For services export, the UK has been India's biggest market within the EU, followed by Germany and France.

Apart from trade in goods and services, the EU is also a major investor in India. The Union's share in India's total FDI approvals during January 1991 to December 2005 was around 25 per cent. These investment approvals rose from US$78 million in 1991 to US$2.314 billion in 2001. From 2001, there was a further increase in investments from the EU. Between April 2000 and June 2012, cumulative FDI inflow from the EU countries amounted to US$ about 43 billion which was about 25 per cent of total FDI inflows into India during this period. This was more than the combined American and Japanese FDI. During the same period, the UK was the EU's top investor in India, followed by the Netherlands, Cyprus, Germany and France.[3]

The FDI, however, has not been only in one direction. Indian FDI in the EU soared to about €10 billion in 2007. Since then it has declined significantly. This suggests that negative economic news about the Eurozone economy has had an adverse affect on Indian investments in the EU. According to some estimates, between 2000 and 2007, around 900 Indian companies invested about US$12 billion in EU Member States. This constituted about 76 per cent of Indian greenfield investments abroad in developed countries. The UK has been a major attraction for Indian companies with more than 500 Indian companies investing around US$ 9 billion between 1990 and 2007. The Netherlands and Cyprus are other main destinations. The majority of earlier investments in the UK have been in the service sector. In recent years, there have been major investments in the manufacturing sector as well.[4] Apart from greenfield investments, Indian companies have been actively involved in overseas acquisitions. According to some estimates, 306 Indian firms were involved in 596 acquisitions worth US $47 billion between 2000 and 2008 in the developed world. Out of these acquisitions, European deals represented more than 50 per cent in value terms.

On the recommendations of the High Level Trade Group (HLTG), which was set up under the Joint Action Plan in 2005, it was agreed at the seventh summit in 2006 at Helsinki that both sides move towards negotiation for a broad-based trade and investment agreement. Both sides agreed that negotiations could begin on the following issues:

(a) *Trade in Goods:* (i) achieving elimination of duties on 90 per cent of tariff lines and trade volume within seven years of the entry into force of the agreement; and (ii) modalities for the treatment of sensitive products including review clauses and partial liberalisation.

(b) *Trade in Services:* (i) ensure substantial sectoral coverage measured in terms of number of sectors, volume of trade and modes of supply. No mode of supply should be excluded; and (ii) provide for the elimination of substantially all discrimination between the parties.

(c) *Investment:* (i) improve market access and provide for national treatment to investors; (ii) ensure that host and home states retain their right to regulate; (iii) foster transparency by clarifying the regulatory framework; (iv) aim at freeing the flow of payments and investment-related capital movements; and (v) seek to facilitate the movement of investment-related natural persons.

(d) *Public Procurement:* Competitive Procurement Regime.

(e) *Technical Regulations:* Cooperation on Technical Barriers to Trade (TBT) and Sanitary and Phyto-Sanitary Measures (SPS).

(f) *Intellectual Property* (IP) and Geographical Indicators (GIs) coverage to IP and GIs in any future agreement.

(g) *Competition Policy:* Agreement on framework in any future agreement.

(h) *Dispute settlement* (DS) and provision of DS mechanism.

It is clear from the agenda that India and Europe are aiming at not just a simple free-trade agreement but a much larger pact which includes services, intellectual property, public procurement, competition policy, etc. In the beginning, both sides were more ambitious. It is now being realised, however, that it was perhaps better to "do the doable" first and go for comprehensive agreement later.[5]

Despite the environment being conducive to a trade deal, governments on both sides have been remarkably slow in negotiations: three deadlines have already been missed and more than a dozen rounds of negotiations have taken place alternatively in Brussels and Delhi. The 14th round of negotiations was held in Delhi in December 2011. At the 9th India-EU summit in France in 2008, leaders agreed to conclude the agreement by 2009 and double their trade in five years.[6] At the 11th summit in Brussels, both sides fixed a mid-2011 deadline to conclude negotiations. After missing another deadline, the 12th in Delhi in February 2102 reiterated that "negotiations on an ambitious and balanced package are now close to completion" and both sides would "monitor the progress of these negotiations for an early conclusion."[7]

The FICCI has expressed concerns that all items of export interest to India, like leather, textiles and garments, may not get covered under the FTA being negotiated with the EU. It suggested the expansion of scope of the pact to cover 95 per cent of merchandise goods.[8] The Communist Party of India (Marxist) asserts that unless details of the agreement are discussed by the Indian Parliament, no commitments should be made. The Politbureau of the Party warns that "such FTAs can turn out to be much more damaging for the livelihoods of our farmers, workers and other sections of the working people than the WTO agreements".[9] Already a campaign group led by trade unions and non-profit organizations has asked the government to halt the talks.[10] A serious campaign has argued that the proposed India-EU FTA would stop flow of cheap drugs to the developing world.[11] Similarly, the domestic industry lobby, the Society of Indian Automobile Manufacturers (SIAM), argues that the proposed deal would kill investments and technology inflow and jeopardise the targets set under the government's own Automotive Mission Plan.[12] Therefore some domestic opposition, the difficult global economic situation and developments on other bilateral economic pacts have already affected India-EU FTA negatively. Despite, compelling reasons for a broad based deal, negotiations have been extremely slow. The global slowdown in recent years also affected these talks negatively. In these circumstances, the major challenge facing policy makers is to conclude negotiations before the thirteenth India-EU summit. For this to happen, however, strong political will is needed from both sides since on balance, both India and the EU stand to gain much more from the agreement than they stand to lose In fact, the trade deal has turned into a litmus test for the commitment of both sides to the strategic partnership.

The Eurozone Crisis and India-EU Economic Ties

India-EU economic relations have also been greatly influenced by internal European economic developments. In the last two decades, the process of European economic integration has undergone tremendous changes. The establishment of the Economic and Monetary Union (EMU), the arrival of the Euro as well as enlargement of the EU to 28 Member States was best viewed in the context of its overall trends towards globalisation. The advent of the Euro also completed the Single Market, which had already ensured the free movement of goods, services, people and capital in the EU. After its successful launch in 1999, the Euro also became the most tangible symbol of a common 'European identity'. It also strengthened the image of Europe worldwide. After decades of success, however, many Eurozone economies are discovering that a single monetary policy in the absence of a single fiscal policy is not working. Despite promises of static and dynamic efficiency gains as a result of a single currency, the Eurozone's economic performance in the last decade has been relatively slow.

After an impressive performance in the last decade, many 'peripheral' economies in the Eurozone are facing a serious debt crisis. The European sovereign debt crisis has grown into one of the biggest challenges the EU has faced in recent times. After Greece, Portugal and Ireland, Italy, Spain and Cyprus are also showing dangerous signs of financial and economic instability. To tackle the issue, the European political elite have initiated several unprecedented measures. Along with the IMF, Eurozone Member States provided financial support to affected countries in the form of pooled bilateral loans. This included a €120 billion package to Greece; €85 billion assistance to Ireland; and €78 billion financing for Portugal. A second bailout package for Greece worth €109 billion has also been agreed upon with easier repayment terms from the private lenders. In so doing, the EU has effectively abandoned the 'no bailout' clause of the

Lisbon Treaty. They also first established the €440 billion European Financial Stability Fund (EFSF) and then expanded it into a €780 billion EFSF. Its mandate is to raise funds in capital markets to provide loans to euro area member states which are experiencing difficulty in obtaining financing at reasonable rates. The EFSF may also intervene in the primary debt market. To strengthen economic policy coordination in the euro area, Member States have also agreed to a European semester and the Euro-Plus Pact. They have further decided to establish a permanent crisis-resolution mechanism, the European Stability Mechanism (ESM) in order to safeguard the euro and financial stability in Europe. The ESM will build on the existing EFSM by mid-2013. There are also discussions about the creation of common Eurobonds backed by all 17 Eurozone countries.

Despite all these measures, the situation remains murky. European attempts to run a common monetary policy without a single fiscal policy is not working. There are reports of the possibility of Greece's exit from the Eurozone. The euro may not collapse but there is a serious possibility of a eurozone break-up, with one or more countries voluntarily abandoning the single currency or forced to exit. Already the European Council has agreed to amend the Lisbon Treaty to provide a legal basis for a permanent mechanism to resolve Eurozone sovereign debt crisis. Now European policy-makers are working on a long term plan to establish a European System to guarantee bank deposits, a banking union, fiscal Integration and common Eurobonds. The President of the European Central Bank (ECB), Mario Draghi, has declared that the ECB would do "whatever it takes to save the euro". Under its new plan, the Outright Monetary Transactions (OMT) scheme, the ECB has pledged to buy unlimited quantities of debt of up to three years in maturity. To qualify, a country would have to accept associated conditions, i.e., promise to make certain economic reforms.

Despite these measures, soon the EU might face a situation where a country leaves or is forced to leave the economic and monetary union. This is going to be a highly challenging situation for the EU, both legally and practically. ECB studies have shown that while negotiated withdrawal would perhaps be possible, unilateral withdrawal will be highly controversial and forced expulsion would be almost impossible. The global economic slowdown as well as the crisis in the Eurozone has definitely affected India-EU trade and investment relations. Trade ties have not affected much as Germany, the biggest economy in the EU and India's largest trade partner in Europe was doing relatively well in the last two years. Latest reports, however, indicate that even German economy is also slowing. Moreover, there has been significant decline in Indian investments to Europe in the last three years.

India-Poland Economic Ties

While looking at India's past relations with the CEE, current negotiations on the broad based trade agreement with the EU and continuing financial crisis within the Euro zone, India Poland ties have experienced both negative and positive trends. Positive trends are coming from high economic growth within Poland and India as well as possibility of bilateral trade deal between India and the EU. Negative sentiments came from initial transformational recession in Poland and now from continuing Eurozone crisis. As shown in Table 1, India -Poland trade has grown to about US$ 1.5 billion annually and is growing on an average about 23 per cent per year in the last four years. This is remarkable in the view of declining economic growth both in Europe and in India.

Table 1: India-Poland Trade, 2007-08 to 2011-12 (In Million US $)

Year	2007-2008	2008-2009	2009-2010	2010-2011	2011-2012
EXPORT	447.45	518.45	421.13	666.22	787.00
%Growth		15.87	-18.77	58.20	18.13
IMPORT	189.46	266.12	387.29	386.04	643.47
%Growth		40.46	45.53	-0.32	66.69
TOTAL TRADE	636.92	784.56	808.42	1,052.25	1,430.47
%Growth		23.18	3.04	30.16	35.94
TRADE BALANCE	257.99	252.33	33.84	280.18	143.53

Source: Export Import Databank, Ministry of Commerce, Government of India.

In addition to trade, two way investments are also happening. According to Indian embassy in Poland, major Indian investors in Poland include Arcelor Mittal, Videocon, Escorts Ltd, Strides Arcolab, Reliance Industries, Ranbaxy, Essel Propack, Zensar Technologies Ltd, Tata Consultancy Services, HCL Technologies, Infosys etc. Similarly, Polish companies that operate in India include Toruńskie Zakłady Materiałów Opatrunkowych (TZMO) in Dindigul (hygiene sanitary products), Can-

Pack Poland in Aurangabad (metal packaging) and Geofizyka TORUN (oil extraction/ exploration).

Another major area of cooperation is defence. This cooperation is facilitated by 2003 Agreement on Military Cooperation. Main areas of cooperatin are tanks, Air/missile defense systems and BMP infantry combat. Overall, Poland would like to invest in Indian sectors like mining, mining machinery, power industry, heavy engineering, waste management, defence industry, pharmaceuticals, food processing, tourism, etc. Similarly Indian companies may be looking new opportunities in areas such as textiles, agriculture, food processing, information technology, infrastructure and tourism.[13] To facilitate economic cooperation both the governments have also signed many agreements which include Agreement on Promotion and Protection of Investments (1996); Agreement on Avoidance of Double Taxation (1981); Agreement on Cooperation in Science and Technology (1993); Agreement on Defence Cooperation (2003); and Agreement on Economic Cooperation (2008).

Conclusion

Poland is an important country within new Europe with whom India had excellent relations during the socialist period and continues to have very close ties. It seems that the importance of Poland is still not fully realized by Indian policy makers. This is a major country representing "new Europe" within the EU. The Polish economic transformation to a market economy in the early 1990s coincided with the Indian economic reforms. The Polish model of economic transformation is generally seen as successful experiment. In the last one decade, the country has been one of the highest growing economies in Europe and its economic linkages with India have grown significantly in the last few years. Despite economic problems with the Eurozone economies, Poland is very positive about its future within the broader European project. So if there is any major breakthrough in the proposed India-EU broad base trade and investment agreement, India-Poland economic ties will witness significant positive impact. In Fact, India should seriously consider signing a Strategic Partnership with this major country from Central and Eastern Europe. This will balance India's relations within the EU where it has special partnerships with the UK, Germany and France from the western part of the continent.

Endnotes

1   For details of all 12 summits and related documents http://eeas.europa.eu/ delegations/india/eu_india/political_   relations/strategic_partnership/index_ en.htm

2   Unless otherwise indicated, all figures used in this article are from various publications of the Indian Ministry of Commerce and Industry and Reserve Bank of India.

3   For details see Gulshan Sachdeva, "India-EU Economic Ties: Strengthening the Core of the Strategic Partnership" in Luis Peral & Vijay Sakhuja (eds), *The EU-India Partnership: Time to Go Strategic* (Paris: EUISS, 2012).

4   For details, see Jaya Prakash Pradan, *India's Emerging Multinationals in the Developed Region,* Munich Personal RePEc Archive Paper No. 12361, http:// mpra.ub.uni-muenchen.de/12361/1/MPRA_paper_12361.pdf   (Accessed November 29, 2013).

5   Suman Modwel and Surendra Singh, *The EU-India FTA Negotiations: Leading to an Agreement or Disagreement,* Occasional Paper No.32, New Delhi: ORF, February 2012.

6   India EU Set to Ink Trade Pact by 2009, Set 100 Bn Euro Target', *The Economic Times*, 28 September 2008. http://economictimes.indiatimes.com/ News/Economy/Foreign_Trade/India-EU_to_ink_trade_pact_by_2009_set_ 100_bl_Euro_target/articleshow/3541388.cms (Accessed   November 29, 2013).

7   India EU Joint Statement, 10 February 2012, http://eeas.europa.eu/india/ sum02_12/docs/20120210_joint _statement_en.pdf (Accessed November 29, 2013).

8   'FTA with EU Must Cover 95% Goods for Real Benefit to India', *Business Line*, 26 September 2008. Available at: http://www.thehindubusinessline.com/ blnus/14261831.htm (Accessed 29 November 2013).

9   See Press Statement by the Politburo of the Communist Party of India (Marxist) on the proposed India-EU Free Trade Agreement, http://cpim.org/ statement/2008/09272008-india-eu%20fta.htm (Accessed November 29, 2013).

10 Amid Protests, EU India Talks Begins Today, http://www.livemint.

com/2009/03/16222358/Amid-protests-EU   India-trade.html   (Accessed November 29, 2013).

11   Sarah Boseley. "Does EU/India Free Trade Agreement Spell the End of Cheap Drugs for Poor Countries?," *The Guardian (UK),* February 10, 2012.

12   Pankaj Doval,. "Auto Industry Against Inclusion in India-European Union Free Trade Agreement," *The Times of India,* May 16, 2012.

13   For details see Alok Rashmi Mukhopadhyay and Sebastian Zukowski, "Poland and India: Bracing for a Strategic Partnership?" IDSA Comment, December 27,   2010,   http://www.idsa.in/idsacomments/PolandandIndiaBracingfora strategicpartnership_armukhopadhyay_270910 (Accessed   November 29, 2013).

Chapter 6

Economic Dimensions of Indo-Polish Relationship: Analysis of Trade Patterns

Sangeeta Khorana

Introduction

Poland and India share a common past as economic and political partners - both countries have a history of socialist economy and experienced nationalisation of the industry. There have, however, been major changes in India and Poland over the last 20 years following political transformation in Central and East Europe (CEE) when Poland joined the European Union (EU) in 2004 and introduced the free market economy model. During this period, India gradually moved from the planned economy model to phased liberalisation, which was achieved by initiating targeted trade liberalisation reforms in 1990s that integrated India with the world economy. As a result of fundamental changes to the economic structures in India and Poland, and guided by the common aim to increase their presence at the global level, economic and trade ties between the partners has grown. The economic relationship has, in particular, received a renewed impetus after Poland's membership to the EU. Both countries have echoed their common interest in promoting the economic dimension of the relationship and recognised the potential that partner countries hold for each other. India perceives Poland as "an additional gateway to the EU single market and a potential market for new investments", and Poland aims to use the growing economic partnership "as an opportunity to enhance and expand Polish firms presence in India".

The genesis of Indo-Polish relationship, which is partly economic and strategic in nature, can be traced back to 1972 when the Indo-Polish Mixed Commission on Economic, Trade and Technical Scientific

Cooperation was established. Economic activity has particularly intensified in the last two decades, and non-currency payment in trading exchange was introduced in 1995 which on the one hand, resulted in a dramatic decline in Polish exports to India and increased imports from India on the other, thus leading to a negative trade balance on the Polish side. In May 2006, the Agreement on Economic Cooperation was signed in Warsaw and this constituted the legal basis for the working of Indo-Polish Mixed Commission. Since 2007, India and Poland as EU Member State, have been involved in negotiations for a bilateral Investment and FTA. Negotiations for an agreement are still on-going, and it is expected that talks will be finalised by the end of 2013. The proposed FTA, which is in line with the *Global Europe* strategy (2006), emphasises EU's aim for a new generation of FTAs that extend beyond present agreements and build towards future multilateral negotiations. The proposed EU-India FTA, thus, is guided by the EU's policy for a FTA which is in line with the letter and the spirit of the WTO Agreements, i.e. comprehensive in scope and deep in terms of level of commitment, in both goods and services.

This chapter examines the economic dimension of the relationship between India and Poland and highlights the changing pattern of trade and deepening economic ties between the partners in recent years. It examines how the pattern of merchandise trade has changed, comments on economic indicators and looks into factors driving India's phenomenal performance, which is primarily attributed to bold incremental economic reforms in trade, industrial policies and the financial sector in 1980s and 1990s. In doing so, it focuses on the growing importance of trade as an economic dimension of Indo-Polish relationship and presents evidence on how the pattern has evolved over time. The chapter also comments on the growing foreign investments and how this is becoming an important part of the Indo-Polish relationship. Finally, there are some concluding thoughts on how trade between India and Poland can be fostered.

An Overview on Economic Indicators: Poland

In 2013, Poland was 33ʳᵈ largest country in the world and 6ᵗʰ largest in the EU[1]. In terms of gross domestic product (GDP), Poland ranks 9ᵗʰ biggest economy in the EU and 23ʳᵈ in the world at 2011 GDP at current prices in US$-denominated terms[2].

Table 1: Country Statistical Profile: Poland 2013

	Unit	2004	2005	2006	2007	2008	2009	2010	2011
Production and income									
GDP per capita	US$ current PPPs	13 010	13 786	15 077	16 759	18 024	18 926	19 908	..
Gross national income (GNI) per capita	US$ current PPPs	12 641	13 516	14 693	16 160	17 660	18 270	19 239	..
Household disposable income	Annual growth %	1.7	1.5	4.5	4.6	4.0	4.8	2.7	..
Economic growth									
Real GDP growth	Annual growth %	5.3	3.6	6.2	6.8	5.1	1.6	3.9	4.3
Net saving rate in household disposable income	%	5.5	5.9	6.1	4.6	-0.3	6.8	6.4	..
Gross fixed capital formation	% of GDP	6.4	6.5	14.9	17.6	9.6	-1.2	-0.4	8.1
Economic structure									
Real value added: agriculture, forestry, fishing	Annual growth %	7.0	0.3	-4.3	-4.1	-1.7	9.1	-4.1	-0.3

	Unit	2004	2005	2006	2007	2008	2009	2010	2011
Real value added: industry	Annual growth %	10.9	3.5	9.9	10.0	6.0	1.3	7.3	6.3
Real value added: services	Annual growth %	3.1	3.4	4.9	11.3	7.5	-4.6	3.3	1.2
Trade									
Imports of goods and services	% of GDP	39.8	37.8	42.2	43.6	43.9	39.4	43.5	45.9
Exports of goods and services	% of GDP	37.5	37.1	40.4	40.8	39.9	39.4	42.2	44.8
Goods trade balance: exports minus imports of goods	Bln US$	-14.4	-12.2	-16.1	-25.4	-38.6	-10.5	-17.1	-19.7
Imports of goods	Bln US$	88.2	101.5	125.6	164.2	210.5	147.1	174.1	203.0
Exports of goods	Bln US$	73.8	89.4	109.6	138.8	171.9	136.6	157.1	183.3
Service trade balance: exports minus imports of services	Bln US$	0.1	0.7	0.7	4.8	5.0	4.8	3.1	6.1
Imports of services	Bln US$	13.4	15.5	19.9	24.2	30.5	24.2	29.6	31.0

	Unit	2004	2005	2006	2007	2008	2009	2010	2011
Exports of services	Bln US$	13.5	16.3	20.6	28.9	35.5	29.0	32.7	37.0
Current account balance of payments	% of GDP	-5.3	-2.4	-3.8	-6.2	-6.5	-4.0	-4.6	-4.3
Foreign direct investment (FDI)									
Outward FDI stocks	Mln US$	..	..	..	..	..	29 304	39 029	50 044
Inward FDI stocks	Mln US$	..	..	..	..	..	185 182	201 003	197 538
Inflows of foreign direct investment	Mln US$	..	..	8 864	5 410	4 413	4 701	5 488	5 870
Outflows of foreign direct investment	Mln US$	..	..	19 599	23 582	14 833	12 936	8 861	15 165
Not available									

Source: OECD Fact Book Statistics, OECD Fact Book 2013

The above data indicates that in terms of 2012 GDP growth rate, Poland ranked 5ᵗʰ among 27 EU member states, falling behind the three Baltic States and Slovakia[3]. Among OECD countries, Poland has been the best growth performer through the global economic crisis. However, with the European economy grinding to a halt following planned fiscal retrenchment, the Polish real GDP growth slowed down to 2.45-3 per cent over 2012. European Commission estimates show that Polish GDP growth may further slow down by 1.1 per cent in 2013 but it is expected to accelerate to 2.2 per cent in 2014. What is particularly striking about Poland is the substantial inflow of EU funds, which on the one hand has contributed to modernising transport infrastructure, and on the other, generated stimulus from domestic macroeconomic policies through exchange-rate depreciation and effective prudential regulation of the financial system. The spill over effects of infrastructure development is evident in Poland's real GDP, which since 2011 has been mainly driven by private consumption and public investment, especially in the construction sector. This sector is estimated to have grown by 4.3 per cent in 2011-12, exceeding OECD estimates of potential growth of about 3-3.5 per cent.

According to GUS data on Poland's trade, the growth in Polish exports exceeded import growth rate in 2012. PLN-denominated exports in current prices were PLN 597.1 billion, which was higher by 6.9 per cent year on year basis. Imports also increased by 2.4 per cent year on year basis, hitting PLN 638.3 billion. As a result of higher export annual growth rates, Poland's foreign trade deficit declined to PLN 41.2 billion in the end of December 2012, compared with PLN 64.6 billion in December-end 2011. Poland also stands out as an important destination for FDI among other CEE countries. According to UNCTAD data, accessed at the beginning of July 2013, FDI inflows to Poland between 2006 and 2011 were US$ 94.9 billion and this was the highest in the region (compared to the Czech Republic at US$ 36.8 billion, Hungary at US$ 26.1 billion in the same period).

An Overview on Economic Indicators: Poland

Trade data suggests that India's merchandise trade increased exponentially in the last decade, from US$ 95.1 billion in 2000-01 to US$ 620.9 billion in 2010-11 and this increased to US$ 793.8 billion in 2011-12. At the same time, India's share in global exports and imports increased from 0.7 per cent and 0.8 per cent, respectively in 2000 to 1.7 per cent and 2.5 per cent, respectively in 2011. India's ranking, in the list of exporting and importing countries, improved from 31 and 26 in 2000 to 19 and 12, respectively in 2011-12. Data released by the Indian government shows that India's total trade as a percentage of the GDP increased from 28.2 per cent in 2004-5 to 43.2 per cent in 2011-12, and that India's merchandise exports as a percentage of GDP increased from 11.8 per cent to 16.5 per cent during the same period[4]. The services sector has been a main driver of India's phenomenal growth rates, making a contribution of over 65 per cent to overall economic growth. Industry and agriculture sectors follow, with a share of 27 per cent and 8 per cent, respectively. Data shows that India's services export growth has been faster than that of merchandise exports with the export of services growing at the compounded annual growth rate (CAGR) of 23.6 per cent during 2001-02 to 2011-12, while merchandise exports grew at CAGR of 21.4 per cent during the same period[5].

The analysis of main trading partners shows that historically India's main export markets were EU-27 (9.9 per cent of total exports), the United Arab Emirates (13.4 per cent), the United States (11.0 per cent) and China (6.5 per cent). This has, however, changed and in 2011-12, following market diversification by Indian exporters after the global crisis. Region-wise, while India's exports to Europe and America declined, its exports to Asia in particular to GCC and Africa increased. In the case of India's exports to the EU, there has been a marginal rise in the share of primary products and petroleum products and a fall in the share of manufactured goods[6]. With regards to composition of trade, services trade surplus as a percentage of GDP increased from US $29.5 billion or 3.1 per cent in 2006-07 to US $54 billion or 4.7 per cent in 2008-09 following increase in software and IT exports, as well as considerable growth in transportation, travel and business services. Similar to Poland, India too benefited from large inflows of capital, both in the form of portfolio investment and FDI. Thus, India remains a success story, having enjoyed high annual real GDP growth which averaged over 8.4 per cent between 2006-07 and 2010-11, and this is mainly attributed to strong domestic consumption and private investment. But India's GDP growth rate has declined in each of the successive quarters between the fourth quarter of 2010-11 and the fourth quarter of 2011-12. Current estimates by the Finance Ministry (2013) project GDP growth to be at 5 per cent for 2013-14, and it is expected to improve to 6 per cent in 2014-15. Table 2 presents an overview on India's economic indicators for 2004-05 to 2012-13, that demonstrates

India's increasing participation in international trade and other economic indicators.

Table 2: Country Profile: India

Indicators	2004-05	2005-06	2006-07	2007-08	2008-09	2009-10	2010-11	2011-12	2012-13
India's Real GDP Growth Rates (at Factor Cost 2004-05 prices)	6.97	9.48	9.57	9.32	6.72	8.59	9.32	6.21	4.96
Exports (US$bn)	85.2	105.2	128.9	166.2	189.0	182.4	250.5	309.8	291.2
Export % YoY	28.5	23.4	22.6	28.9	13.7	-3.5	40.4	20.9	-6.0
Imports (US$bn)	118.9	157.1	190.7	257.6	308.5	300.6	381.1	499.5	479.6
Imports %YoY	48.6	32.1	21.4	35.1	19.8	-2.6	27.6	30.3	-4.0
Trade deficit (US$bn)	-33.7	-51.9	-61.8	-91.5	-119.5	-118.2	-130.6	-189.8	-188.4
Invisibles (US$bn)	31.2	42.0	52.2	75.7	91.6	80.0	79.3	111.6	112.4
Current Account Deficit (US$bn)	-2.5	-9.9	-9.6	-15.7	-27.9	-38.2	-45.9	-78.2	-69.9
Current Account Deficit (% to GDP)	-0.3	-1.2	-1.0	-1.3	-2.3	-2.8	-2.7	-4.2	-3.7
Capital Account (US$bn)	28.0	25.5	45.2	106.6	6.8	51.6	63.7	67.8	77.6
Capital Account (% GDP)	3.9	3.1	4.8	8.6	0.6	3.8	3.8	3.7	4.1

Indica-tors	2004-05	2005-06	2006-07	2007-08	2008-09	2009-10	2010-11	2011-12	2012-13
Debt Service Ratio	5.9	10.1	4.7	4.8	4.4	5.8	4.3	6.0	4.5
Forex Assets (exc. gold) (US$bn)	135.1	145.1	191.9	299.1	241.6	252.8	273.7	260.9	259.6
External Debt (US$bn)	134.0	139.1	172.4	224.4	224.5	260.9	305.9	345.4	360.4
Short Term Debt	17.7	19.5	28.1	45.7	43.3	52.3	65.0	78.2	83.2
Exchange Rate US$/ Rs. – average	44.3	45.2	40.2	46.0	47.4	45.6	48.1	54.0	54.5

Source: Reserve Bank of India, Central Statistical Organisation, Ministry of Finance, Government of India.

The explanation to India's phenomenal performance is couched in incremental economic reforms in trade, industrial policies and the financial sector in 1980s and 1990s which have received widespread attention[7]. Studies show how India's gradual and incremental reforms to the trade regime reduced reliance on inward-looking import substitution strategy and marked the shift from "license-permit-quota" regime towards a pro-business attitude (Rodrik and Subramaniam, 2005). Some trade liberalisation measures undertaken in 1980s include lowering of tariffs and reduced imports of canalised items, and relaxation of industrial controls. Complementary measures undertaken were de-licensing and broad banding of domestic industries (which allowed firms to switch productions between similar production lines), tax reforms i.e. introduction of Modified Value Added Tax, and relaxation of Monopolies and Restrictive Trade Practices (MRTP) 1969 Act.[8] These reforms allowed India to move cautiously from a protectionist economy towards a controlled market economy, both in terms of disinvestment (privatisation) and opening the market to foreign players (liberalisation). This led to spectacular growth in some sectors, and India's per capita income increased from US$300 to US$1,700 over 1990-2009 and its share in world GDP grew from 4.3 to

5.3 per cent during 1991-2009 (WTO 2011). India is also participating in liberalisation through bilateral trade agreements – it has signed 10 FTAs, 5 preferential trade agreements (PTAs) and these FTAs/PTAs are already in force. Further, India is currently negotiating 17 FTAs, including review/ expansion of some of the existing ones.

Trade Relations between India and Poland: Merchandise Trade

Figure 1 shows the total value of trade in goods between India and Poland, which has grown steadily from US$ 105 million in 1996-97 to US$ 1683 million in 2012-13.

Figure 1: Goods Trade between India-Poland (million US$): 1997-2013

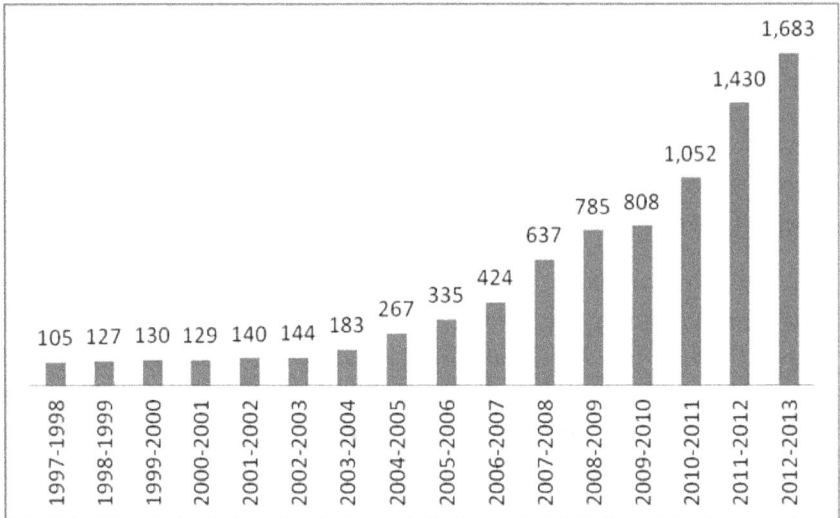

Source: Ministry of Commerce, Government of India.

A closer examination of trade data reveals that trade has grown considerably on year to year basis from 2001 to 2002, registering a consistent increase in the following years with the largest increase in 2007-08. In some ways, 2004 can be seen as a watershed year when Poland joined the EU and this is when trade began to grow between India and Poland. Trade has consistently increased since 2004, except in 2009-10 when trade was adversely hit following the global downturn.

Table 3 presents detailed breakdown of merchandise trade values and annual growth rates between India and Poland over 1996-2013. The total value of trade was US$ 105.29 million in 1996-97, of which Poland's exports to India were US$ 28.70 million and imports to Poland were US$ 76.51 in 1996-97. This increased to 874.87 million and 808.23 million, respectively in 2012-13.

Table 3: Overview on EU-India trade (1996-2013)

Year	EU - India Trade (in US$ million)			
	Export from Poland to India		Import to Poland from India	
	Total value	% growth (with 1996 as base year)	Total value	% growth (with 1996 as base year)
1996-1997	28.780	-	76.510	-
1997-1998	32.700	13.65	87.430	14.27
1998-1999	33.810	3.38	93.060	6.45
1999-2000	38.490	13.87	91.660	-1.51
2000-2001	42.630	10.76	86.220	-5.93
2001-2002	31.390	-26.37	108.310	25.61
2002-2003	38.840	23.73	105.64	-2.46
2003-2004	49.050	26.29	134.21	27.04
2004-2005	90.370	84.22	176.300	31.36
2005-2006	107.810	19.31	226.960	28.74
2006-2007	107.230	8.74	306.570	35.08
2007-2008	189.460	61.61	447.450	45.96
2008-2009	266.120	40.46	518.450	15.87
2009-2010	387.290	45.53	421.130	-18.77
2010-2011	386.040	-0.32	666.220	58.2
2011-2012	643.470	66.69	787.000	18.13
2012-2013	874.870	35.96	808.230	2.7

Source: Ministry of Commerce, Government of India.

Figure 2 presents the evolution of export-import pattern between India and Poland over 1996-97 to 2012-13.

Figure 2: India-Poland Trade

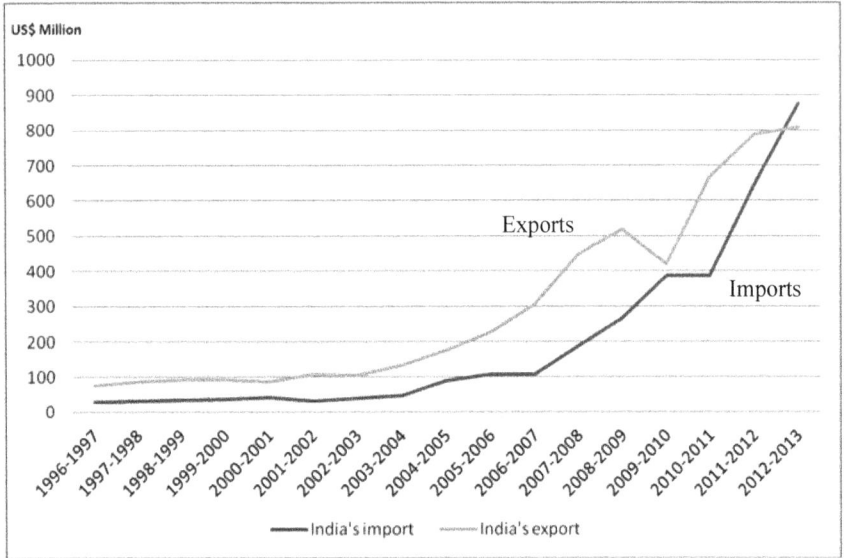

Source: Ministry of Commerce, Government of India.

Further detailed analysis (Figure 3) of India's trade patterns over 1996-97 and 2012-13 with Poland reveals that the main export items are vehicle accessories and parts (HS 87), organic chemicals such as cefadroxil and its salts, ibuprofane, nifedipine, ranitidine, salts of phenyl glyc (HS 29); Apparel and clothing (HS 54) such as T-shirts, singlets and other vests of cotton, knitted or crotcheted; Cotton (HS 61); and, Iron and steel products of width =>600 mm (HS 72).

Figure 3: India's Exports to Poland (1996-2012)

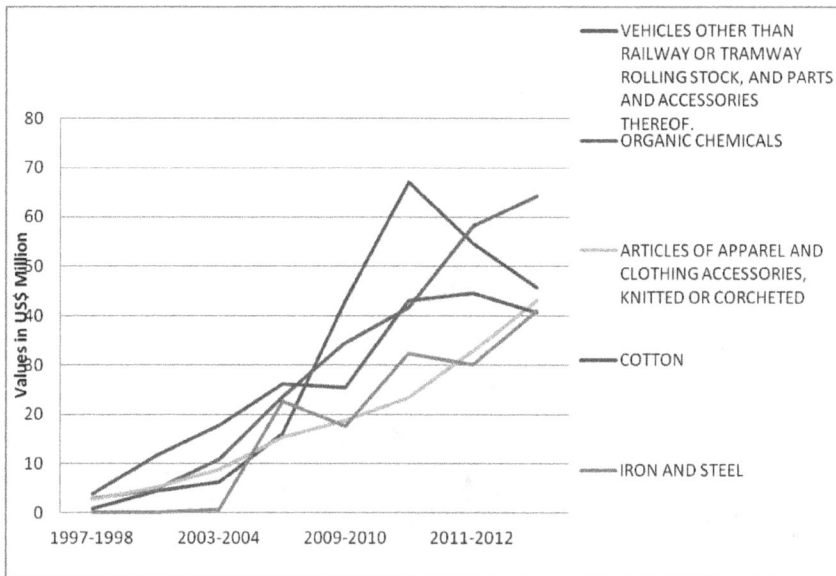

Examination of trade patterns for 2012-13 reveals a shift in the composition and pattern of India's exports to Poland over 1996-97 to 2012-13. Figure 4 demonstrates the share of top 10 exports of India to Poland for 2012-13, and shows that top three export performers for India are: telephones for cellular use dominate (53 per cent), organic compounds (26 per cent) and granite (24 per cent).

Figure 4: India's Export - top 10 Commodities in 2012-2013

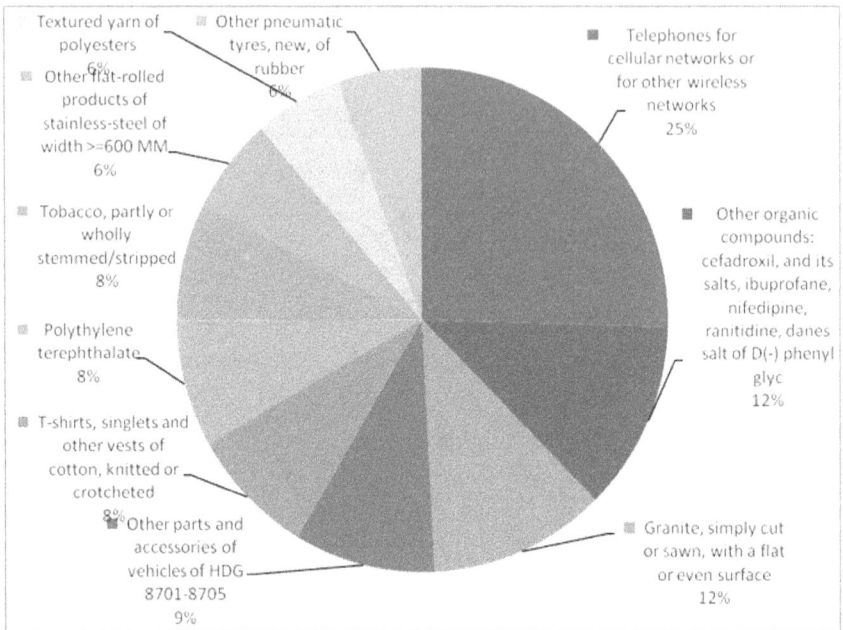

Source: Ministry of Commerce, Government of India.

Table 4 presents the composition of India's exports to Poland in value terms with HS classifications.

Table 4: Composition of India's Exports to Poland (2011-12)

HS Code	Commodity	Value (million US $)
851712	Telephones for cellular networks or for other wireless networks	53.29
294200	Other organic compounds: cefadroxil, and its salts, ibuprofane, nifedipine, ranitidine, danes salt of D(-) phenyl glyc	25.61
680223	Granite, simply cut or sawn, with a flat or even surface	24.27
870899	Other parts and accessories of vehicles of HDG 8701-8705	19.41

610910	T-shirts, singlets and other vests of cotton, knitted or crotcheted	17.43
390760	Polythylene terephthalate	17.04
240120	Tobacco, partly or wholly stemmed/ stripped	15.96
721990	Other flat-rolled products of stainless-steel of width >=600 MM	12.73
540233	Textured yarn of polyesters	12.30
401199	Other pneumatic tyres, new, of rubber	11.56

Source: Ministry of Commerce, Government of India.

The analysis of India's imports (Figure 5) from Poland suggests that ships and boats (HS 89) have registered the highest growth rates over 1996-97 to 2012-13, followed by nuclear reactors, boilers (HS 84). Other sector that has performed consistently is iron and steel (HS 72).

Figure 5: India's Imports from Poland (1997-2012)

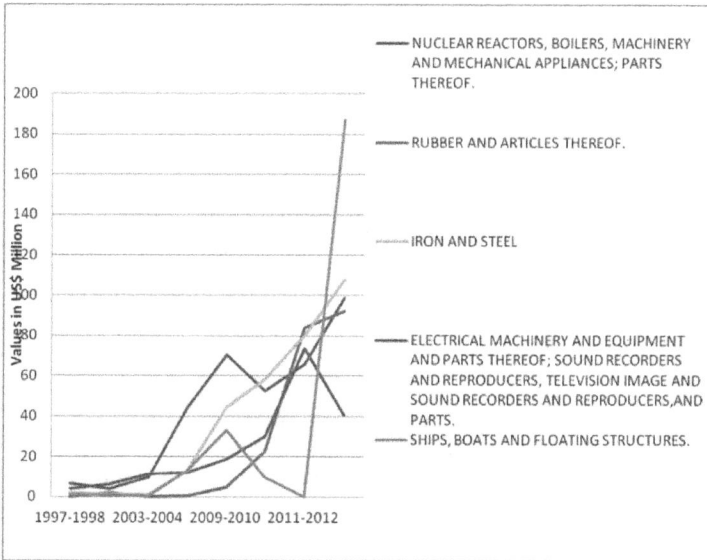

Source: Ministry of Commerce, Government of India.

Trade values are indicative of the changing patterns of trade between India and Poland (Table 5). A closer look at the 2011-12 trade data suggests that India imports mainly comprise of coal (US$ 142 million), followed by rubber (US$ 88 million) and cruise ships (US$81 million).

Table 5: India's Imports from Poland (2011-12)

HS Code	Commodity	Value (million US $)
270400	Coke and semi-coke of coal, of lignite or of peat, whether or not agglomerated; retort carbon	142.22
400219	Styrene-butadiene rubber "SBR"; carboxylated styrene-butadiene rubber "XSBR", in primary forms or in plates, sheets or strip (excl. latex	88.21
890110	Cruise ships, excursion boats and similar vessels principally designed for the transport of persons; ferry-boats of all kinds	80.54
890800	Vessels and other floating structures for breaking up	71.76
720449	Other waste and scrap of iron or steel "ECSC"	51.58
840820	Compression-ignition Internal Combustion Piston Engines for Vehicles	37.71
890590	Light-vessels, fire-floats, floating cranes and other vessels, the navigability of which is subsidiary to their main function (excl. dredgers, floating or submersible drilling or production platforms; fishing vessels and warships)	34.74
722511	Flat-rolled products of silicon-electrical steel, of a width of >= 600 mm, grain-oriented "ECSC"	33.21
271019	Other petroleum oils and oils obtained from bituminous minerals and preparations	20.73
710691	Silver, incl. silver plated with gold or platinum, unwrought (excl. silver in powder form)	14.12

Source: Ministry of Commerce, Government of India.

On the basis of the current pattern of Indo-Poland trade, it is apparent that Polish companies can cooperate in sectors in which Polish firms enjoy a comparative advantage. These sectors include: mining industry (building structures; providing machinery, equipment and services), traditional power plants industry, military industry, oil and gas prospecting, pharmaceutical industry, medical apparatus and equipment, machinery and equipment of agricultural food processing industry and environmental protection (installations and technology transfer). The most significant seems to be mining given that Poland has vast experience in mining, especially in deep underground mining.

Cross Border Investments

Similar to merchandise trade, the number of direct investments has also registered an increase with Indian and Polish companies making investments in each other's economy. For instance, the total value of India's investments in Poland is estimated at US$ 44.3 million (2009). In recent years, main investments by India have been in the informatics services sector and BPO i.e. technology, IT, outsourcing, cars, machines and steel production. Polish investments in India have also grown, and at the end of 2009 the Polish National Bank estimated total investments in India at US$ 141.8 million. Polish companies have invested in 12 power industries plants and 13 mining structures have been installed in India, including chemicals, machines, metallurgical, food and construction industries, as well as Rajdoot motorcycles factory and Escort tractors factory. These include two joint-ventures - Bella India (hygienic materials) and factory for aluminium beverages cans – previously mentioned CAN PACK Poland S.A. built in 2009 in Aurangabad. Other investors are: Polmor (Hyderabad, welded constructions, rail industry), VTS (Bangalore, AC equipment systems), Bumar (military industry), Geofizyka Torun (mining industry) and Cenzin (military and special equipment); Zamet cooperates with OFB Calcutta providing huge machines for copper alloy processing.

Other prominent examples of cross border investments include Toruń Bandaging Materials Factory, which produces personal hygiene items and the cosmetics producer iNGLoT, from Przemyśl, which is operating on the franchise model. Data shows that Polish investments in India were €35.6 million in 2008, and that Polish investments exceeded the value of Indian investments in Poland (€28 million). Polish companies also participate in on-shore oil and gas prospecting (Poszukiwania Nafty i Gazu Nafta Piła and Geofizyka Toruń). Furthermore, Polish Minister of Defence Bogdan Klich and the Indian Ambassador to Poland Deepak Vohra signed an agreement in May 2011 for mutual military cooperation.

Indian companies that have invested in Poland are: Infosys, Zensar, HCL, Essel Propack and Wipro. However, some of the foreign investments are not direct – a prominent example is that of Mittal Steel which has an investment of around US$ 1 billion and controls 70 per cent of the Polish steel industry but is registered in the UK. Main Indian investors in Poland are: Videocon Group (with an annual turnover of more than US$4 billion); Farmtrac Tractors Europe, which produces agricultural machines in Mrągowo; Reliance Industries Group, which produces textured polyester fibre in Zielona Góra; Essen Propack, a leading producer of plastic packing tubes; Varroc engineering, producing steel parts and sub-assemblies for the automotive branch in Warsaw; Berger Paints, making internal heating systems for buildings in Żywiec; Novo Tech, Ltd, producing automotive parts and accessories and consumer products from polymers; Lambda Therapeutics research; and the pharmaceuticals firm Arcolab.

In the IT sector, prominent investors include: VSNL; Teleglobe international Holdings; KPIT; Cummins, Zensar Technology; HCL Technologies; Infosys; WIPRO; Intelenet Globar and CSS. Indian companies such as Tata Consultancy Services, Wipro Technologies, ZenSar and Videocon have already set up their base in Poland.

Other notable investments include those by: Tata Motors, Tata Tetley, Sylvania Havells India, Jindal Stainless Ltd and pharmaceutical firms, such as Glenmark Pharmaceuticals Ltd and Ranbaxy that have representatives in Poland. Further, the Confederation of Indian Industries (CII) has sent delegations to Poland to explore economic opportunities in various sectors. In 2008, the Indo-Polish Chamber of Commerce and Industry (IPCCI) was instituted to protect and represent the interests within the range of economic activity and to promote economic relations between India and Poland.

The Way Forward

Trade data substantiates that economic cooperation between India and Poland has grown. Recent examples of cooperation which will boost the economic dimension of the relationship include an agreement on avoiding double taxation and Audio-Visual Co-production Agreement that will enable filmmakers from both countries to work together on joint projects. More recently in 2013, India Expo Fair was held and this event is envisaged to be the platform for future business and economic exchanges between Poland and India. Such activities will promote and increase levels of trade between the trading partners. With regards to future trade possibilities and given the needs of the Indian market and Polish export possibilities, the greatest opportunity for bilateral cooperation is apparent in the energy sector for the supply of replacement parts, renovation for modernisation of power plants built by Polish firms, and renewable energy. Other potential sectors include coal mining for planning, sinking of shafts, supply of machines and extraction equipment, enriching and sorting coal, mining and oil and gas exploration. Sectors such as food processing, health care (medical equipment, including hospital equipment), the chemical industry (specialised chemical products, paint components) and defence (Polish military technology) are also potentially important for Polish India trade.

The unlimited possibility that the growing Indian market offers complemented by booming demand of Indian consumers is the mantra for success of Polish firms as this could leverage growth and help firms to achieve economies of scale. At the same time, the deepening of economic cooperation at a strategic level between Poland and India could give both Polish and Indian entrepreneurs a new outlook on business and acquaint them with operating models in each others' economies. From a business perspective, the underlying strengths of Indian and Polish firms are entrepreneurship, adaptability, creativity, and the capacity to combine diverse elements, which support business expansion and give firms a unique competitive edge in gaining market access in the current environment. Both India and Poland simply cannot miss out on an opportunity for greater economic cooperation. For this, however, India needs to accelerate and continue the second generation of reforms to utilise the emerging opportunities effectively and, in doing so needs to address difficult and divisive political issues, to accelerate growth that will prevent India from losing its magic.

Endnotes

1 CIA. The World Fact Book, 2013.

2 International Monetary Fund. World Economic Outlook Database, 2013.

3   Eurostat (2013). Trade Statistics, Directorate of Foreign Trade, Brussels.

4   Ministry of Finance, Government of India. *Economic Survey, 2013.*

5   Ibid

6   (DGCIS, 2012) Directorate General of Foreign Trade {DGFT} (2012), Ministry of Commerce and Industry, New Delhi, http://dgft.delhi.nic.in/ Director General of Commercial Intelligence and Statistics {DGCI&S} (2012), Ministry of Commerce, Government of India.

7   I. J. Ahluwalia. 'Productivity and Growth in Indian Manufacturing,' (New Delhi: Oxford University Press, 1991); M. S. Ahluwalia. 'Economic Reforms in India Since 1991: Has Gradualism Worked?' *Journal of Economic Perspective*, 16, 3, 2002. pp. 67–88; V. N Balasubramanyam. 'India: Trade Policy Review', *The World Economy*, 26, 9, 2003, pp. 1357-1368; B. S. Bosworth, Collins and A. Virmani. 'Sources of Growth in Indian Economy', NBER Working Paper No. 12901, 2007, National Bureau of Economic Research; V. Srivastava, 'The Impact of Liberalisation on Productivity and Competition: A Panel Study of Indian Manufacturing, 1980–89' (New Delhi: Oxford University Press, 1994); P. Trivedi, A. Prakash, and D. Sinate, 'Productivity and Major Manufacturing Industries in India: 1973-74 to 1997-98', Development Research Group Study No. 20, Department of Economic Analysis and Policy, Reserve Bank of India. 2000; A. Virmani, 'Sources of India's Economic Growth', ICRIER Working Paper No. 131, Indian Council for Research on International Economic Relations (ICRIER), New Delhi, 2004; B. N. Goldar. 'Trade Liberalisation and Manufacturing Employment: The Case of India', International Labour Organisation, 2002/34, 2004.

8   Major liberalisation reforms in 1991, which were part of an IMF structural adjustment package and designed to combat balance of payments imbalances, included further trade liberalisation through reduction in average tariffs (from 125 per cent to 40 per cent over 1990-96) and statutory peak rate of tariffs (from 400 per cent to 50 per cent over 1991-96), as well as relaxation of capital flows and exchange rate mechanism. In addition, quantitative restrictions (QRs) were abolished for capital and intermediate goods, with a negative list for imports of consumer goods and agricultural products. Automatic approval for foreign direct investment (FDI) up to 51 per cent was initiated, which was relaxed in subsequent years. Finally, entry conditions were loosened for firms under the MRTP Act.

Chapter 7

Economic Transition in Poland and India:
Not So Different Story?

Karina Jędrzejowska

Introduction

At the end of 20th century, Jeffrey E. Garten, in his book *The Big Ten Emerging Markets,* pointed out that the fastest growing economies in the world, most of them still classified as developing countries, were gaining more and more influence on global trade, finance and politics. The ten potential economic powers were: Mexico, Brazil and Argentina in the Americas; China, India, Indonesia and South Korea in Asia; Poland and Turkey in Europe; and South Africa, in Africa. Ruchir Sharma, in his book *Breakout Nations,* analyzed major emerging markets in search of the "next economic miracles". Although at the first glance countries in question appear to have little in common, most of them have succeeded in deep economic and political system transformation over the last two decades that enabled them to join either the ranks of advanced economies or become biggest and most influential emerging economies in the world[1].

The beginnings of the shift of power in the world economy can be traced back to the 1980s and the early 1990s when many developing countries, including India, were introducing neoliberal reforms. Simultaneously, adoption of market reforms in Poland worked as a catalyst for the collapse of the Soviet-style command economic system of Central and Eastern Europe (CEE) and the Soviet Union. The magnitude and intensity of this change were historically unprecedented. The transformation affected hundreds of millions of people directly and, indirectly billions more. Although the reversal of economic system was in its beginnings, painful and long-lasting for many countries, it led to improvement in competitiveness, better access to international financial markets, and improved living conditions. Major transition economies, most of them mentioned by Garten and Sharma, have managed to overcome initial difficulties and today gradually increase their positions in global economy[2].

This chapter attempts to analyze economic transition experienced by Poland and India. It discusses Polish and Indian economic transformation after 1990 and the possible similarities and differences in the reform processes in both countries. It deals with justification for the comparison and presents theoretical background for economic transition. It also focuses on the reforms in Poland – their initial conditions, policies applied and economic outcomes.

Justification for Comparison

Poland, as a representative of Central and Eastern European EU members, and India as a representative of developing countries of South Asia, are not directly comparable entities. They differ *inter alia* in terms of level of economic development, degree of income inequality, per capita GNI or trade links. However, based on GDP growth and transition towards market economy over the last 20 years, reform processes in both countries show some similarity.

India's growth and change of position in the global economy are compared mostly to China's experience, while Poland's performance is usually compared to other post-communist economies. Poland is the most populous of the former Soviet satellites. With approximately 38 million people, and with approximately 121,000 sq. miles, Poland boasts one of the largest territories in Europe. Therefore, Poland can be seen both as a large market for goods and services, and a strategic location for Indian companies that wish to do business in the CEE and the EU. Similarly, India represents a fast growing market, with a population exceeding 1.2 billion and a territory of 1,269,219 sq. miles, second only to China. Economic reforms have made the region attractive for foreign investment, including investment from Poland. Growing trade linkages between India and Poland confirm mutual economic interests [3].

The justification for comparing Poland and India is twofold; first, Poland and India, though different in size of their economies, belong to the big emerging markets of the 21ˢᵗ century. They have shown immense progress over the last two decades in integrating with and upgrading within the global economy. Despite increased level of integration with global markets, both countries managed to avoid the major effects of the subprime crisis of 2008. Secondly, both countries used to have highly centralized economies and have adopted programmes of stabilisation and structural adjustment in the 1990s. Yet the way these programmes were implemented differs greatly, and the political history of the two regions could not have been more different[4].

There are also some further similarities to be named. These include the fact that the past development strategies in both Poland and India have reached their limits and led to economic decline and stagnation. In both cases previous policies included strong state intervention and highly protectionist policies that resulted in problems of inefficiency and inability to compete internationally, and a relatively high level of foreign indebtedness. What constitutes the major difference is the fact that Poland used to be an authoritarian communist regime, while India is counted among democracies since its independence. Nevertheless, India was until 1990 the country with a huge public sector, second only to communist countries like Poland.

Both India and Poland were affected by the more or less direct consequences of the global debt crisis of the 1980s. One of the global consequences of the crisis was a wave of market-oriented economic reforms in most developing regions of the world. Although the reforms were strongest and most sustained in Latin America, and almost a decade later in post-communist countries of CEE, it was very much a global phenomenon. Stabilisation and "structural adjustment" had become the primary preoccupation of policy makers across the "global South" and post-Soviet area, even though the implementation level and outcomes of reforms varied greatly. In the wave of economic opening also India, "the giant archetype of a closed, import-substituting economy among developing countries, embarked on a process of economic liberalization in 1991", and Poland opened up after the communist regime collapsed[5].

Even if the direction of reforms in Poland and India was convergent, there were several differences as well. In many respects, Poland, just as the Soviet Union and its other satellites, was an "above normal developing country". It had achieved high level of industrialisation and urbanisation, provided universal public health care and education, and was characterised by low income inequalities. At the same time, however, Poland was showing endemic shortages, queues and black markets. The system was unable to identify and satisfy elementary needs of the population, not to mention the near-famine conditions and high inflation shortly before transition in 1989. Yet in spite of initial difficulties, contemporary Poland is a high-income economy, member of the EU, WTO and OECD. Despite being considered an advanced economy and economic leader of the region, it is however rarely listed as one of potential economic powers of the world.[6]

In contrast to the above, pre-reform India was in most aspects a typical developing country. At the first glance it had distinguished itself from most representatives of the "global South" by its vast population and high level of absolute poverty. Moreover, until June 1991 India was considered the most autarkic non-communist country in the world. According to the IMF, India was among the most heavily regulated economies in the world characterised by economic nationalism, high level of external protection and internal regulation. Therefore, the economic policy reforms launched in 1991 constitute a watershed in India's economic history. These reforms reflect a deep reorientation in India's development strategy which included change in the role of state in economy, shift towards free market and integration with the world economy. After over 20 years since the beginning of liberalisation, India belongs to the most influential and fastest growing countries in the world, but it is still troubled by problems typical for the developing world. According to Martin Wolf "because of the vast size of its population (expected to become the largest in the world in the 2020s), India is set to become a 'premature superpower' that is, a still relatively poor country, with huge domestic problems, yet one with a big impact upon the globe"[7].

On Economic Transition and Beyond

There is no single definition of economic transformation. Economic transformation and economic transition usually mean the process of change of an economic system. It could be transition between different types of capitalist systems (e.g. from liberal to social capitalism), but in most cases there is a deeper transition happening: from planned economy towards free market. Often economic reforms are reinforced by parallel transformation of political system[8].

The process of reconstruction of an economic system is complex, demanding and to some degree – risky. Economic system transformation requires far reaching changes in resource allocation, redistribution and pricing mechanisms. Additionally, changes in resource management, technological upgrading, changes in resource ownership structure and major restructuring of financial system are needed. These changes may result in temporal losses of productivity, output, income and employment. Therefore, even though in the long-term there might be a net positive gain, economic transition usually leads to a short-term decline in social and economic conditions.[9]

Any larger project of deep economic reform usually consists of two phases: economic stabilisation and structural adjustment. Stabilisation (or macroeconomic stabilisation) is a short-term programme, usually lasting up to two years. It is oriented towards alleviating macroeconomic imbalances such as high inflation, fiscal deficit or balance-of-payments problems. Usually changes in exchange rate regime are implemented at this time. As for the structural adjustment, it is a long-term process aimed at increasing efficiency and competitiveness of the economic system. It addresses not only the consequences of the imbalances, but their causes as well. It involves shift in the balance between state and the market and the relation between national and world economy. Such developments were present both in India's and Poland's case.[10]

The direction and form of transition are country-specific, as they are influenced by the country's economic and political environment, current policies of major international organisations, economic policies implemented by major economic powers, and recommendations provided by economic theory. Beginning from the 1980s, most economic transformations included "jump to the market" as Joseph E. Stiglitz called it, and were more or less directly based on the neoliberal paradigm promoted by the international financial institutions (IFIs) such as the IMF and the World Bank.[11]

Based on the experience of the late 1980s reforms in Latin American countries, the neoliberal policies were summarised by John Williamson in ten points which were later popularised as the so called Washington consensus. The consensus promoted free market policies and macroeconomic stabilisation. It encouraged trade liberalisation and deregulation. It favoured market regulatory process over state intervention typical for Keynesian and Marxist style policies preferred at the time by most developing countries. According to the neoliberal scheme, it was the market and not the state that was in charge of economic growth. Moreover, macroeconomic stability obtained by the means of fiscal discipline, tax reforms and export growth was believed to be the prerequisite necessary for accelerated growth and economic development.[12]

There can be no doubt that market forces constitute a major factor in world development. Yet the minimisation of state intervention and the extension of the private sector do not always guarantee sustainable economic development. After almost three decades of structural adjustment it is a common knowledge that neoliberal reform packages did not always bring long-term growth in countries that decided (or were forced) to follow this line. According to the major architect of the transformation in Poland, Leszek Balcerowicz, the process and outcome of economic transition depend on the initial conditions (e.g., level of human capital, level of indebtedness), the transition strategy, and the conditions prevailing during this process. These conditions influence the final outcome of any transition. They include also political context which influences quality of policies and their implementation. Similar conclusions were reached in the 1996 World Development Report entitled *From Plan to Market*, which stated that differences in economic performance between countries implementing the Washington consensus were associated mostly with "good and bad" policies, in particular with the progress in macroeconomic stabilisation and outcomes of opening of the economy.[13]

The 1990s had witnessed numerous economic liberalisation attempts in various regions. Even though the economic transformations of the 1990s are usually associated with the CEE post-communist countries, the liberalisation took place also in Asia, Africa and continued in Latin America. Many closed economies that previously relied heavily on state-owned enterprises, extensive economic planning and import substitution started opening up and liberalising in order to integrate with global economy and accelerate growth. As already mentioned, despite major differences in their history, level of human development or political systems (e.g. Poland was under repressive communist government, while India was a mature democracy), the policies implemented by most developing countries in the late 1980s and 1990s show many similarities.[14] In particular, during the transition the primary aim was to reduce the role of the state in the economy and allow market mechanism to allocate resources. This policy was exemplified by the financial liberalisation, privatisation, fiscal austerity, competitive exchange rates, lowering of import barriers, and deregulation of foreign direct investment.[15]

Before 1989 most communist economies followed an economic model that included state intervention in almost all aspects of economic activity. The Soviet-type economic system was characterised by almost complete dominance of state ownership and enterprise, state monopoly of foreign trade, inconvertible currencies, obligatory central planning, and a monolithic banking system (the Central Bank usually acting as a "Monobank"). Consumer prices and wages were determined by the government, and some consumer goods and services rationed. The resulting resource allocation was highly inefficient and created many distortions (also of political nature), which later contributed to the fall of the regimes.[16]

Despite existence of the Washington consensus, the economic system transformation in the former Soviet bloc did not have many theories and recommendations to rely directly on. Therefore, the exact transition strategy was a *de facto* experiment with unknown results. It was only the Latin American experience with macroeconomic stabilisation and structural adjustment that provided some instructions for Poland and other transition economies. The parallels in situation between Latin American heavily indebted economies and Soviet satellites included: implementation of economic reforms under condition of high indebtedness and weak market economy, introduction of structural adjustment in state-dominated economy with suppressed market mechanisms, necessity to reform financial systems (inclusive exchange regime) and legacy of decades of import substituted industrialisation.[17]

Although they differ in diverse country-specific aspects, the policies adopted by transition economies can be divided into two schemes: a "shock therapy" approach and the "gradual therapy" approach to economic restructuring. "Shock therapy" refers to the immediate stabilisation. It includes rapid introduction of a package of monetary and fiscal measures to tighten the expansion of domestic credit, abandon price controls, eliminate inflationary pressures and subsequently introduce privatisation programmes.[18] According to its advocates, the rapid liberalisation allows to avoid painful and costly period, "when the old centrally planned economy is not working already, while the new market one is not working yet"[19]. On the other hand, gradual approach includes sequencing of reforms and step-by-step opening allowing domestic enterprises to adjust to the new conditions. Gradualists stressed the example of China, arguing that the lack of recession and high growth rates is the direct result of the gradual approach to economic transformation.[20]

However, even the shock therapy does not lead to a "minimalist state". As Berríos states: "almost all of today's strong economies developed under states which played active roles in fostering and protecting economic activity. Although free-market reforms supposedly entail a dramatically reduced state from the economic arena, in reality they also require a strong state to enforce measures that have high social costs. While democracy may require capitalism, capitalism does not necessarily require democracy."[21] Here it is worth mentioning that the fact of India being a democracy is considered a major reason for its cautious and gradualist approach to reforms. Reforms in India were sequenced over a period of time – from one budget to the next in order to minimise social cost of the process, while Poland experienced with "shock therapy".[22]

Poland's Reconstruction of Market Economy

Poland was the first country in the CEE to reestablish a market economy. After almost a quarter of century since introduction of the market-determined reform packages, Poland's transformation can be regarded as a success. Yet compared to other post-communist economies of the region, Poland's performance might not be the best. Slovenia, Slovakia, Czech Republic (and until economic crisis of 2008 Hungary) have shown comparable (or maybe better) economic and social indicators, but it has to be remembered that Poland is the biggest economy among them. Moreover, it is the only country in the region (and the EU as well) that managed to avoid recession in the aftermath of the subprime crisis of 2008.[23]

Similar to other socialist countries, Poland represented a command-type of economic system which was "dominated by the state sector, characterised by heavy industrial concentration, equipped with distorted prices due to massive price subsidies and controls, geared to import substitution, and deprived of both internal and external competition".[24] Most of market institutions were non-existent or heavily distorted. To makes matters worse, there was no proper central bank, banking system was subordinated to the government, and there was no stock exchange. Additional fiscal burden constituted extensive and inefficient social protection system which distinguished the CEE communist countries from transition economies in other regions. These facts indicate that the scope of transformation was deeper than economic transformation in Latin America or Asia.[25]

Given the level of ineffectiveness in the centrally planned economies, much of the advice given to Poland by the IMF indicated that any form of gradual reform was unlikely to be successful, and the transition should have been carried out in a swift manner. As Poland was the first country in the region to introduce market reforms, other CEE countries benefited from both successes and mistakes of the Polish policy makers. Moreover, the neoliberal reforms imposed on the region were not uniform, and subject to modification by the countries implementing them. Therefore, Poland stands as an example for a model "shock therapy", while reforms in Czech Republic and Slovakia were slower, Hungary implemented more gradualist approach, and the latest reformer of the region, Slovenia, implemented what is believed to be a fully gradualist programme.[26]

Although some market reforms in Poland date back to 1988, it is the implementation of the reform package known as the Balcerowicz Plan (named after the finance minister and deputy Prime Minister of the time) that started in Janurary 1990 that marks the beginning of Poland's economic transformation. The plan is often regarded as synonymous to the shock therapy in Poland. The goal of this market-oriented reform package was transformation of the Polish economic system to what Professor Balcerowicz often referred to as "western-style economy". The core elements of the Balcerowicz Plan included: macroeconomic stabilisation, liberalisation (end of central planning, deregulation of prices and capital controls, integration with the world economy), institutional restructuring and privatisation. The first part of the stabilisation programme consisted of policies aimed at curbing inflation and reducing excessive domestic demand.[27] These included abolishment of the centrally controlled prices and trade controls; reduction in government spending to reduce the budget deficit (this involved mainly reduction of subsidies for ineffective state-owned companies); application of a tight credit policy to reduce the money supply; introduction of positive and high real interest rates; application of restrictive income policy with a tax on wage increases (so called "popiwek"); weakening the public monopoly; introduction of the internal convertibility and devaluation of the Polish currency – the Zloty; reform of the banking system; and investment policy oriented towards foreign capital. The plan was backed by the financial and technical assistance provided by western governments and the IMF. After reaching the stabilisation further development of market institutions was intended[28].

Dismantling of the centrally planned system in Poland has proven more difficult than initially expected, and the economic contraction of the 1990-1992 exceeded the projections. Only during the first year the GNP declined by 11.6 per cent, real wages by 30 per cent, and employment by 6 per cent. Industrial production sank by 24 per cent. Economic problems were intensified by political instability. Since 1989 (when the Communist Party surrendered power) until 1995 Poland had seven Prime Ministers, four governments and four national elections. The main reason behind social discontent was growing unemployment, declining real incomes and a striking lack of understanding of market forces in the mostly Soviet-raised society[29].

In spite of the above problems, by the year 1993 economic growth in Poland was restored. After 1991 over 90 per cent of the total volume of transactions was conducted at market prices. Between 1990 and 1993 more than a million of new private enterprises were registered. By the end of 1993 the share of employment in the private sector exceeded 60 per cent, while the private sector contribution to the GDP exceeded 50 per cent, and was fuelled by gradually rising foreign investment inflow. Simultaneously Poland had rebuilt its tax system by introducing western-style corporate and personal income taxes (1992), and the value added tax (1993). Successful negotiations with the Paris and London Clubs, the level of foreign liabilities sank by over 50 per cent[30].

Major changes of the 1990s were applied for the banking sector. In the first half of 1989, Poland started to depart from the typical socialist banking sector with its monobank structure, and no clear separation between the banking system and the state budget. Until 1993 the number of commercial banks increased from 7 to over 80, not to mention a growing number of credit unions and cooperative banks. In 1991, nine large commercial banks were turned into joint stock companies, that were later privatised (mostly sold to foreign investors)[31]. These changes required introduction of non-banking financial institutions and a stock exchange that "had to be built totally from scratch" and opened in July 1991[32].

It is disputable whether the Polish transformation can be regarded as a full success. Some authors, including Grzegorz W. Kołodko, stress that some opportunities have been wasted, and the success was only partial. Nevertheless, Poland's position as a developed economy today is unquestioned. Despite rising costs of a welfare state and ageing society, its status as a modern social market economy does not seem threatened. Poland benefits from the membership in the European Union, yet it has not adopted the common currency yet and the fiscal troubles are increasing. Moreover, despite joining major international economic organisations, Poland is not directly involved in the works of G20 and very rarely considered as a major economic power[33].

India's Liberalisation Experience

When Poland was on its way towards social market economy, India was gradually introducing neoliberal reforms and creating environment for deepening private sector that enhanced changes started in Indian economy a decade before and enabled India to join the ranks of major economic powers. In order to see the scope of this change it is enough to mention that only in the early 1980s China and India together accounted for less than 5 per cent of global output. By the end of 2012, these two emerging economic powers were producing over 20 per cent of world GDP. Despite several indicators classifying India as a developing country (e.g. the level of poverty in India seems appealing), India today is among most influential economies in the world being a member of bodies such as G20 or the Basel Committee[34].

Yet not so long back, India's economic prospects had not seemed positive. Its economic performance during the first three decades since independence in 1947 was often referred to as the "Hindu" rate of growth, a term indicating a disappointing but not disastrous economic outcome. India in the major part of the second half of the 20th century, was regarded as an example of wasted opportunities and failed development strategies. Until 1991, policy-makers in India followed policies that closed the economy to international trade, promoted development of inefficient industries under state guidance, and restricted private economic activity with controls and bureaucratic impediments[35].

India's state-centric development strategy was consistent with the development agenda of the 1950s and 1960s. Similar to the Soviet economies, the centrepiece of India's development strategy was modernisation through industrialisation. State-owned enterprises were created to take leading roles in all industries and sectors viewed as central to the industrialisation program, including steel, chemicals and engineering, as well as trade and finance. India attempted to develop somehow against global markets, aiming at economic independence achieved through more or less successful import substitution. Contrary to the Soviet model, however, private property was not discarded, and India succeeded in building stable democratic institutions [36].

Focus on industrialisation resulted in underdevelopment of agriculture that had been partially overcome due to the innovations brought about by the green revolution in the 1960s. Yet again these were above all government initiatives that made possible creating the institutional and physical infrastructure necessary to improve agricultural productivity, including irrigation works and dams, rural roads and markets, credit cooperatives, price support programs and extension programs for education and training of farmers. A final, significant dimension of development strategy aimed at improving the well-being of the population by public provision of minimum levels of basic services in such areas as health and education[37].

Despite massive efforts, India's growth remained low, and the country could not overcome its major problems such as high levels of poverty, suppressed private sector or inefficient fiscal policy. By the 1980s, India's relative lack of success became more apparent, with the cumulative impacts of decades of higher growth in East and Southeast Asia. Even though India grew more rapidly in the 1980s than in previous post-independence decades, it lagged far behind China in its growth rate. Simultaneously India's foreign debt increased and it experienced trade and current account deficits in the 1980s. These deficits were financed through resorting to the foreign exchange reserves and commercial borrowing abroad which led to further growth of indebtedness[38] .

Economic problems of the 1980s marked first phase of the India's economic transformation. Although the transition is believed to have started in 1991, its roots can be traced back to the aftermath of the oil crisis of the 1970s; the reform programme was launched in 1984 as a result of balance-of-payments crisis caused by persistent fiscal deficits. The crisis increased in 1991 which accelerated introduction of neoliberal policies in India. The government of India had to resort to the IMF and the World Bank rescue package. It resulted in adopting New Economic Policy that included liberalisation and deregulation, inclusive signing GATT agreement in 1994 as part of the package[39].

Whereas Poland has seen a radical change of political system and return to democracy after fall of the communist regime, there was also change in government orientation in India after the 1989 election. It was then that the Congress Party took control and P.V. Narasimha Rao became the Prime Minister. Similar to the Polish case, the major task of reforming the economy was given to the Finance Minister, Manmohan Singh. As Leszek Balcerowicz became a symbol of the transition in Poland, it will be Manmohan Singh who may be regarded as its equivalent for India – "the main instigator of the long-overdue liberalization of the Indian economy"[40].

Reforms undertaken in India after 1991 included both internal and external policy. In result the balance between protectionism and economic openness has been altered in favour of the latter. The new neoliberal policies included opening for international trade and investment, deregulation of the private sector, initiation of privatisation, tax reforms and typically for such programmes inflation-controlling measures. Deregulation of the private sector included dismantling of the so called 'License Raj'. In the course of reforms, industrial licensing was significantly reduced (except 15 industries of strategic or environmental importance), and only six industries were reserved for public sector. Moreover, Indian Rupee was sharply devaluated by 20 per cent, and gradually made fully convertible on the current account. Yet contrary to the CEE countries, the capital controls in India were sustained.[41] Openness to international trade was increased through tariff reductions and replacement of import quotas by tariffs, and the reduction of industrial licensing.[42]

Another aspect of India's reform constitutes transformation of its financial system. Until the beginning of the 1990s, the condition of the Indian financial sector could be described as a classic example of financial repression. The sector was characterised *inter alia* by administered interest rates, dominant public ownership, strong entry barriers limited competition, severe credit constraints on the private sector, especially in the absence of external financing.[43] The reforms included introduction of private commercial banks and greater reliance on market forces. Establishment of the Securities and Exchange Board of India (SEBI) in 1992 shifted the capital markets regulation from the government authorities[44]. Simultaneously monetary policy used to be (similarly to the communist economies) subservient to the fiscal policy has been liberalised. Yet the Reserve Bank of India (RBI) has not decided to pursue monetary policy based on direct inflation targeting, and even today the RBI cannot be regarded as a fully independent central bank[45].

The economic stabilisation in India had as its immediate objective restoration of macroeconomic stability and access to international financial markets. In the 1990s and subsequently, India has been one of the fastest growing economies in the world[46]. Parallel grew its involvement in international trade. Yet the results of Indian reforms can be considered as mixed. On the one hand, India managed to build a substantial and diversified industrial base. It is far more developed – both in economic and human development terms than most countries of Africa, the Middle East or even parts of Latin America. On the other hand, when compared with other countries that went through the process of "late industrialisation" and catching-up, as e.g. South Korea, Brazil or China – the gap remains wide in spite of the post-1991 reform and later development[47].

Conclusion

Examples of economic transformation from all developing regions show that economic transition can be extremely elaborate and complex, and in some cases a devastating process. Most of transition economies have experienced contraction in real GDP, contraction in real per capita incomes, high unemployment and high inflation. Simultaneously, almost quarter of a century after economic liberalization – countries like Poland or India have managed to alter their international position and increase global influence.

The historical background and implementation, "shock therapy" versus gradualism, of reforms in both countries presented in the chapter differ, yet the foundations of the change show great similarities. Both countries introduced programmes encompassing radical changes in fiscal and monetary management, development and promotion of private sector, opening of economies, privatisation of ineffective state-owned enterprises, and construction of a modern financial sector. It is obvious that the story of reforms in Poland and India presented in the chapter is not complete. Both countries also experienced significant transformation of their societies and politics. This shift was accompanied by changes in the global economic order that further influenced internal policies.

The outcomes of the economic reforms of the 1990s were not always entirely successful, and some of the processes such as privatisation in Poland, cannot be regarded as completed. Nevertheless, the 20-year perspective economic transformation proved successful in the long-run. Both countries managed to improve their economic condition and standards of living of their societies to some extent. Looking at purely economic dimension, it is worth noting that India is counted as one of major economic powers today in spite of showing some features of a developing country. Poland, on the other hand, can be counted among advanced nations, yet its global influence compared to India remains limited.

Endnotes

1   Jeffey E. Garten. *The Big Ten: The Big Emerging Markets And How They Will Change Our Lives* (New York: Basic Books, 1998); Ruchir Sharma, *Breakout Nations. In Search of the Next Economic Miracles* (London: Allen Lane, an imprint of Penguin Books, 2012).

2   Demetrios Giannaros. "Twenty Years After The Economic Restructuring Of Eastern Europe: An Economic Review", *International Business & Economics Research Journal*, Vol. 7, No. 11, 2008, p. 35; Rubén Berríos, "Economic Transition in Poland: the relevance of the Latin American experience", *Revista de Economia Política*, vol. 15, no. 4, 1995, p. 112.

3   Jan P. Muczyk, "Stages of transition from a planned to a free-market economy: Poland as a case study", online publication, 1998 http://www.sba.muohio.edu/abas/1998/poland1.pdf (Accessed September 4, 2013), p. 1.

4   Giovanni Andrea Cornia. "Economic Integration, Inequality and Growth: Latin America vs. the European Economies in Transition", DESA Working Paper No. 101, January 2011, p. 20.

5   Dani Rodrik. "Understanding Economic Policy Reform", *Journal of Economic Literature*, Vol. 34, No. 1. (Mar., 1996), p. 10; Dani Rodrik & Arvind Subramanian, "From "Hindu Growth" to Productivity Surge: The Mystery of the Indian Growth Transition", IMF Working Paper WP/04/77 (May 2004), p. 10.

6   D. Mario Nuti. "The Former Soviet Union after Disintegration and Transition",

TIGER Working Paper Series No. 117, Warsaw, January 2010, p. 4.

7 Martin Wolf. *India in the World*, in Shankar Acharya & Rakesh Mohan (Eds), *India's Economy Performance and Challenges. Essays in Honour of Montek Singh Ahluwalia* (New Delhi: Oxford University Press, 2010), p. 370; Baldev Raj Nayar. "Political Structure and India's Economic Reforms of the 1990s", *Pacific Affairs*, Vol. 71, No. 3 (Autumn 1998), pp. 335.

8 Revilla-Diez, Schiller and Zvirgzde. "Similarities and Differences of Institutional Change in ENP and Other Catch-Up Countries", WP5/14 Search Working Paper, January 2013, p. 4.

9 Demetrios Giannaros. p. 37.

10 Baldev Raj Nayar. p. 338.

11 Jeffrey D. Sachs. *Poland's Jump to the Market Economy* (Cambridge, MIT Press, 1993).

12 Revilla-Diez, Schiller and Zvirgzde, "Similarities and Differences of Institutional Change", p. 4-5.

13 Leszek Balcerowicz. "Poland: the economic outcomes", *Economic Policy*, December 1994, p. 72; Revilla-Diez, Schiller and Zvirgzde. "Similarities and Differences of Institutional Change", p. 6; Berríos. "Economic Transition", p. 125; Vladimir Popov, "Shock therapy versus gradualism: the end of the debate (explaining the magnitude of transformational recession)", p. 3. http://pages.nes.ru/vpopov/documents/TR-REC-full.pdf (Accessed September 4, .2013).

14 Vladimir Popov. p. 8.

15 Kostova Huffman & Johnson. p. 9.

16 D. Mario Nuti, "The Former Soviet Union", p. 2; Sonya Kostova Huffman & Stanley R. Johnson. "Re-evaluation of Welfare Changes during the Transition in Poland", Working Paper 00-WP 255, October 2000, Center for Agricultural and Rural Development, Iowa State University, p. 9; Nirvikar Singh, "India's Development Strategy: Accidents, Design and Replicability", MPRA Paper No. 12453 (September 2008), p. 1.

17 Giannaros, "Twenty Years After", p. 35; Berríos, "Economic Transition", p. 113; Grzegorz W. Kolodko & Michal Rutkowski, "The Problem of Transition from a Socialist to a Free Market Economy: The Case of Poland", *The Journal*

of Social,Political and Economic Studies, Summer 1991, Vol. 16, No. 2, p. 3.

18 Jeffrey Sachs. "Reforms in Eastern Europe and the Former Soviet Union in Light of the East Asian Experiences", CASE Research Foundation Working Paper, May 1995, p. 8;

19 Vladimir Popov. p. 3.

20 Muczyk. "Stages of transition", p. 2; Berríos, "Economic Transition", p. 120.

21 Berríos. "Economic Transition", p. 114.

22 Baldev Raj Nayar. pp. 355-356.

23 Ruchir Sharma. "Breakout Nations", pp. 99-104.

24 Balcerowicz. "Poland: The Economic Outcomes", p. 73.

25 Balcerowicz, "Poland: the economic outcomes", p. 73; Janos Kornai, "The Role of the State in a Post-Socialist Economy", Leon Koźmiński Academy of Entrepreneurship and Management (WSPiZ) and TIGER Distinguished Lectures Series, No. 6, Warsaw, November 2001, p. 11; Sachs, "Reforms in Eastern Europe", pp. 3-4.

26 Berríos, "Economic Transition", pp. 119-120.

27 Poland was the only post-communist economy (except for the former Yugoslavia) facing hyperinflation, most of the actions named above were meant to curb it. The annual consumer price index during the last five months of 1989 exceeded 600 percent, but after just a few months of market opening the it went down to around 250 percent by the end of 1990. Three years later it was already below 40 percent. These numbers can be considered a success as for high-inflation Latin American countries like Chile and Mexico it took up to seven years to reduce three-digit inflation to 15-20 percent. The successful fight with inflation enabled the National Bank of Poland (*Narodowy Bank Polski* – NBP) to run a monetary policy based on the direct inflation targeting already in 1998. See: Balcerowicz, "Poland: the economic outcomes", p. 82.

28 Kostova Huffman & Johnson, "Re-evaluation of Welfare Changes", p. 10; Giannaros, "Twenty Years After", p. 36; Rodrik, "Understanding Economic Policy Reform", p. 34.

29 Kolodko & Rutkowski, "The Problem of Transition"; Berríos, "Economic

Transition", p. 122.

30 Balcerowicz, "Poland: the economic outcomes", pp. 86-89; Kostova Huffman & Johnson, "Re-evaluation of Welfare Changes", p. 10-11.

31 Libor Žídek, "Transformation in Poland", *Review of Economic Perspectives – Národohospodářský Obzor*, Vol. 11, Issue 4, 2011, pp. 253-254.

32 Leszek Balcerowicz. p. 88.

33 This brief report does not cover all aspects of the Polish transformation. Due to the volume limit and requirements such important aspects of the Polish transition as privatization, agriculture and social policy were omitted. For a detailed analysis of Poland's transition see publications by Leszek Balcerowicz or Grzegorz W. Kołodko.

34 Jean Drèze & Amartya Sen, *India. Development and Participation* (New Delhi: Oxford University Press, Oxford India Paperbacks, 2012), p. 66.

35 Rodrik & Subramanian, "From "Hindu Growth" to Productivity Surge", p. 3.

36 Nirvikar Singh. , p. 2.

37 Ibid, p. 3.

38 Baldev Raj Nayar. p. 340.

39 Rodrik & Subramanian, "From "Hindu Growth" to Productivity Surge", p. 37; Anke Hoogvelt, *Globalization and the Postcolonial World. The New Political Economy of Development*, Second Edition, (Basingstoke: Palgrave Macmillan, 2001), p. 152.

40 Vijay Joshi, *Fiscal Stabilization and Economic Reform in India*, in: Isher Judge Ahluwalia & I.M.D. Little (eds), *India's Economic Reforms and Development. Essays for Manmohan Singh*, Second Edition (New Delhi: Oxford University Press, 1998), p. 163.

41 Large net inflows of capital to India have created adjustment challenges. India has decided to continue on employing capital controls on capital movements and running a managed floating exchange rate regime, thereby accumulating large foreign exchange reserves. For more information see: Wolf, *India in the World*, p. 379.

42 Baldev Raj Nayar. p. 336; Rodrik & Subramanian, "From "Hindu Growth" to

Productivity Surge", p. 3.

43 Rakesh Mohan, *India's Financial Sector and Monetary Policy Reforms*, in Shankar Acharya & Rakesh Mohan (eds), *India's Economy Performance and Challenges. Essays in Honour of Montek Singh Ahluwalia* (New Delhi: Oxford University Press, 2010), pp. 151-152.

44 Jaimini Bhagwati, *Indian Capital Markets, 1991-2008*, [in:] Shankar Acharya & Rakesh Mohan (Eds), *India's Economy Performance and Challenges. Essays in Honour of Montek Singh Ahluwalia* (New Delhi: Oxford University Press, 2010), pp. 180-182.

45 Rakesh Mohan. p. 152.

46 Nirvikar Singh Singh. p. 9.

47 Atul Kohli, *State-Directed Development. Political Power and Industrialization in the Global Periphery* (Cambridge: Cambridge University Press, 2004), pp. 285-286.

Chapter 8

Exploring India-Poland Co-operation on Energy and Environment: Opportunities and Challenges

Dinoj K. Upadhyay

Introduction

Protection of environment and access to clean energy are integral parts of the sustainable development strategy in India.[1] Due to population pressure, rapid process of urbanization, 'anthropogenic development employing energy-intensive technologies'[2] and so on, India faces severe challenges of environmental degradation. On the other hand, high economic growth rate is essential for reducing poverty. The country relies on fossil fuels to spur its economic growth. Rising greenhouse gas (GHG) emissions and associated climate change have further aggravated the environmental problems. The projected changes in climate would have severe implications for society and economy. Poor and marginalized sections of the society would be more vulnerable to climate change because they have limited capacity to cope up. Application of clean technology, promotion of renewable energy and enhancement of energy efficiency are crucial elements of a sustainable growth strategy, which will help in protection of environment, proliferation of access to clean energy, enhancing energy security and reducing the threats of climate change.

As one of the most vulnerable countries to climate change as well as an emergent emitter of GHG, India has been endeavouring to balance its economic growth and development trajectory. Having primarily relied on oil, coal and natural gas, India has also been making efforts to diversify its energy imports to minimize the risks associated with energy supply and promote renewable energy. Due to initiatives from the government, private sector and civil society organizations, usages of renewable energy have been gradually expanding. India has emerged as a huge market for renewable energy, efficient energy usages and clean technologies. New Delhi has taken a number of initiatives, particularly National Action Plan on Climate Change (NAPCC) to cope with climate change and promote sustainable development. The NAPCC consists of eight national missions, which combine both mitigation and adaptation measures. The missions under NAPCC are intended to promote solar energy, energy efficiency, sustainable agriculture, sustainable habitat, and strategic knowledge on climate change. The NAPCC provides a policy framework, incentives, and opens huge business opportunities in the areas of renewable energy, clean technology and energy efficiency.

In this context, this chapter aims to analyze India-Poland cooperation in energy, particularly coal, mining and shale gas. While analyzing the policies of India and Poland on global climate regime for emission cuts, the chapter examines how India and Poland can cooperate in areas of environmental protection, renewable energy, clean technology and energy efficiency within the framework of the NAPCC. Finally, it analyzes major challenges for bilateral cooperation between New Delhi and Warsaw.

Rising Energy Demands in India

Sustainable access to clean energy at an affordable price is essential for facilitating high economic growth and promoting social development in India. The Integrated Energy Policy (IEP, 2006) of India states that '*the country would be energy secure when it can supply lifeline energy to all citizens irrespective of their ability to pay for it, as well as meet their effective demand for safe and convenient energy to satisfy their various needs at competitive prices, at all times and with a prescribed confidence level considering shocks and disruptions that can be reasonably expected*'.[3] The IEP also estimated that India is required to grow an 8 per cent to 10 per cent for next 25 years for eradicating poverty and promoting inclusive social development. As an essential for economic growth, India needs to increase its primary energy supply by three to four times and, its electricity generation capacity/supply by five to six times of the 2003-04 levels.[4]

There is a pressing gap between demand and supply of electricity in India. It is estimated that the country has an installed generating capacity of around 1,50,000 megawatt and per capita consumption of 650 units of electricity per annum. *A Report on India's Energy security from TERI* estimates that India has been suffering from huge estimated shortages of around 10 per cent in energy terms and almost 17 per cent in terms of peak demand. Although India achieved only limited success in establishing new oil reserves, it has had considerably higher success in establishing natural gas finds. But the lack of adequate delivery infrastructure has significantly limited the expansion of, and spread of benefits from this source.[5]   The report has critically observed that India's petroleum sector has been beset by inadequate investments in resource development, inefficiencies in production, and inadequate resource allocation for technology development. Petroleum sector has been one of the most difficult sectors to open up for private participation and application of more modern and efficient mining technologies.[6]

India-Poland Energy Cooperation

Energy security has become a crucial element of India's foreign policy. As demand for energy has been ballooning, New Delhi has been constantly exploring possibilities for cooperation with potential partners to make its energy security more robust and dynamic. To put it briefly, Indian energy diplomacy ranges from imports of energy, investment in technological cooperation with energy and technology rich countries. Considering the various aspects of the energy security, there are several areas in which Poland and India can cooperate and develop a mutually beneficial energy partnership.

Coal: Coal remains the mainstay of power generation in India. The IEP states that 55 per cent of electricity has been generated by coal based power plants. *The Expert Group Report on Energy Policy* further points out that coal would be critical for future power generation in India. Coal sector provides immense opportunity for cooperation in terms of mining, technology, equipment to both India and Poland. It is considered that Poland has competitive advantages in the coal sector. Thus, Poland can be helpful in several activities such as underground mining, easy-to-use machines and technologies for the extraction industry in India. Exploring possibilities, energy experts have noted that equipment for coal-fired power plants can also be obtained from Poland. Recent estimates show that Poland has huge coal reserves. It is the world's 10th largest reserves of coal and major Polish coal companies have started exports.[7] Since India's Inc. is not able to meet the demand of coal from domestic sources due to some policy issues, they are looking beyond their usual suppliers like Australia and Indonesia. Indian steel and power companies have started importing coal from far destinations such as Canada.[8] Indian Ministry of Coal has already signed agreement with Poland for cooperation in the coal sector. The Indo-Polish Joint Commission on Economic, Trade, Scientific and Technical Cooperation has identified underground mining, washery construction, thermal power generation, mine safety and rescue as the major areas of cooperation.[9] In an interview, Indian Ambassador to Poland Monika Kapil Mohta said, "there are moves towards tangible cooperation in the coal sector. Preparatory work needs to be done leading up to high-level contact for meaningful talks on coal exports as well as the acquisition of coal assets."[10] The Union Minister of Steel, Shri Beni Prasad Verma visited Poland in October 2013 and had expressed strong desire for cooperation in coal mining and steel sector.[11]

Shale Gas: Shale gas is another emerging area of cooperation between India and Poland. The US Energy Information Administration (EIA) estimates that the top 33 countries are estimated to have around 6,622 trillion cubic feet (tcf) of technically recoverable shale gas resources. It further states that the shale gas reserves are likely to increase as more regions are explored. Based on current reserve estimates and consumption, shale gas reserves could potentially satisfy global gas requirements for the next six decades. According to the latest estimates by the EIA, Poland has the largest technically recoverable shale resources in Europe, which is estimated to be around 187 tcf.[12] Recent technological advancements in hydraulic fracturing and horizontal drilling have made shale gas operations economically viable. The widely dispersed shale gas reserves represent the strong potential to emerge as a major alternative source of energy globally.

Early estimates suggest that India could have around 96 tcf of recoverable shale gas reserves, which would be able to meet its gas demands for two decades. Six basins namely Cambay in the state of Gujarat, Assam-Arakan in the North-East region, Gondawana in central part, KG onshore in Andhra Pradesh, Cauvery onshore and Indo-Gangetic basins have been projected as potential shale gas reserves. India's policy gives permit to Oil and Natural Gas Corp (ONGC) and Oil India Ltd (OIL) to explore shale resources from on land blocks that were allotted to them on a nomination basis before the advent of the New Exploration Licensing Policy in 1999.[13]

Given the state of the supply deficit and heavy reliance on imports, it becomes imperative for India to harness all energy resources, including shale gas, appropriately. The unlocking of domestic shale gas can help India meet its growing energy demand, besides reducing its dependence on expensive energy imports and the energy import bill.[14] Poland is considered to be leader in the extraction of shale gas. Technological cooperation between India and Poland can be useful in the production of shale gas in India. Poland has also taken initiatives in expanding technological expertise; for instance, the Polish Ministry of Environment and the State Mining Authority organised specific training programmes for a better understanding of shale gas operations.[15]

Renewable Energy

Considering the threats of global warming and enhancing access to clean energy, India has taken major steps for promoting grid and off-grid production of renewable energy. Due to favorable policy framework and financial incentives provided by the Government of India, renewable energy sector has emerged as one of the most attractive markets in the world. Renewable sources, for instance, solar and wind can be areas of cooperation between India and Poland.

Solar Energy. The National Solar Mission intends to significantly increase the share of solar energy in the total energy mix while recognizing the need to expand the scope of other renewable. The NAPCC points out, "India is a tropical country, where sunshine is available for longer hours per day and in great intensity. Solar energy, therefore, has great potential as future energy source. It also has the advantage of permitting the decentralized distribution of energy, thereby empowering people at the grassroots level."[16] The Mission document further states that the country is endowed with vast solar energy potential as about 5,000 trillion kWh per year energy incident over India's land area with most parts receiving 4-7 kWh per sq. m per day. The Mission envisions for both technology routes for conversion of solar radiation into heat and electricity, namely solar thermal and solar photovoltacis and has a target of the deployment of 20,000 MW of solar power by 2022.[17] It is proposed in the Mission that a decentralized mechanism for power generation (rooftop installations) and distribution system would be developed in the country.[18]

National Tariff Policy has been amended, making it obligatory for provinces to purchase solar power 0.25 per cent by 2013 and 3 per cent by 2020. 100 per cent FDI is permitted in the renewable energy generation and distribution projects in India. India is one of the most developed renewable energy market and Ernst & Young ranks India as the fourth most attractive country to invest in renewable energy.[19] Polish companies can invest and enter in joint venture with Indian counterparts. Many Polish renewable energy companies such as APS Energia S. A., ASKET Roman Dlugi, Fu-Wi Ltd etc are operating across the world. Their participation in the Indian renewable energy sector would be mutually beneficial for India and Poland.[20]

Wind Energy. India has an installed capacity of 17,365.03 MW wind energy in 2012 and is ranked 5th in the terms of installed capacity after the US, China, Germany and Spain. The country has potential to increase electricity generation from wind. It is estimated that with the current level of technology, the 'on-shore' potential for utilization of wind energy for electricity generation is of the order of 102 GW.[21]

There are mainly three factors which make the wind sector favorable in India. Firstly, India's wind energy potential is about 80,000 MW and there are a few players in the fray. The shift from an accelerated depreciation model to a generation-based incentive, renewable energy purchase obligations for state utilities under the NAPCC and preferential tariffs from state utilities for electricity generated from renewable sources. Secondly, with conventional energy sources like thermal and gas becoming more expensive, the Government is increasing prices significantly. The price of wind power is competitive, more affordable in some cases. Lastly, wind energy is a capital and labour intensive business.[22] European countries such as Germany and Spain are keen in investment and doing business with Indian companies in the wind sector. There are also opportunities for Polish companies to tap the business potential available in the Indian market.

Energy Efficiency

The IEA notes that energy efficiency is 'hidden energy'. Promotion of energy efficiency can save energy which can be distributed to energy deficient sectors. Government of India has taken initiatives to save energy through application of energy efficient appliances. The National Mission on Enhanced Energy Efficiency (NMEEE) has a mandate to adopt a market based mechanism to enhance cost effectiveness of improvements in energy efficiency in energy-intensive large industries and facilities, accelerating the shift to energy efficiency appliances to make them more affordable, providing energy efficiency financing platform and developing fiscal instruments to promote energy efficiency. The NMEEE aims to throw multiple energy efficiency opportunities, estimated to be about Rs. 74,000 crores. It also intends to annual fuel savings in excess of 23 million tons by 2014-25, cumulative avoided electricity capacity addition of 19000 MW and CO_2 emission mitigation of 98 million tons per year.[23]

Clean Technology

India has the fourth largest coal reserves, 285862.21 million tonnes and 55 per cent of electricity is generated by coal. India's IEP 2006 estimates that by 2030, 41 per cent of total commercial energy would be met by coal. Coal scores high on security of supply and competitiveness and will remain a major source of energy for future. But emission from coal-based generation is a matter of serious concern. Clean coal technologies are crucial in improving the quality of non-cooking coal, improving efficiency of coal utilization and reducing carbon dioxide and other pollutant emissions. India and Poland can cooperate at the bilateral and multilateral levels, within the framework of the EU. India and Poland can cooperate in areas such as Joint Technology Development and Induction of Supercritical and Adv-Ultra Supercritical Technology, Emission/Waste Management, Ash Utilization options, Innovative Repair & Maintenance and Re-powering, knowledge sharing through exchange programmes, and promoting manufacturing and testing facilities in India.

India-Poland Cooperation on Environment

Considering the broad and strong political relations between India and Poland, there is immense potential for countries to cooperate to cope with climate change. Poland is member of the EU, but the EU and India differ on the critical issues related to climate change adaptation and mitigation. India and the EU are diametrically opposed to each other on global regime on emission cut. Even Poland does not endorse EU policy on climate change. Poland is against any commitments for emission cut by the EU beyond 2020 unless it is in the framework of the UN agreement. Poland is also not in favor of any climate commitments amidst economic crisis in Europe.[24] There are some crucial areas in NAPCC, in which India would be interested for cooperation with Poland. Agriculture, water management and knowledge and information/research and development sharing, etc are potential areas of cooperation between the two countries.

Water Management

The World Development Report 2009 notes that water is essential for achieving sustainable development as well as MDGs. It further points out that water is linked to the crises of climate change, energy and food supplies and prices, and troubled financial markets.[25] The main objectives of the National Water Mission is to ensure integrated water resource management helping to conserve water, minimize wastage and ensure more equitable distribution both across and within states. The National Water Mission aims to "conservation of water, minimizing wastage and ensuring its more equitable distribution both across and within States through integrated water resources development and management". The five identified goals of the Mission are: (a) comprehensive water data base in public domain and assessment of impact of climate change on water resource; (b) promotion of citizen and state action for water conservation, augmentation and preservation; (c) focused attention to over-exploited areas; (d) increasing water use efficiency by 20 per cent, and (e) promotion of basin level integrated water resources management.[26] The Mission points out the climate change impacts on water sector and highlights the growing concerns.

India's per capita availability of water, on the basis of the 2011 census, has fallen below the global threshold, signaling that the country will have to address conservation needs more seriously amid a growing population and an expanding economy.[27] Per capita water availability was 5, 177 cubic meters in 1951, which has been reduced to 1829 cubic meters and projected to be 1340 and 1140 cubic meters in 2025 and 2050, respectively.[28] India allocated Rs.100 crore during the 12th five-year plan for water recharge, of which Rs. 61 crore has been utilized so far. The Planning Commission has now proposed an accelerated water recharge project in all states during the 13th five-year plan period to scale up conservation.[29] Considering the water crisis across the world, India and Poland should explore possibilities in water management, efficiency in water uses, water saving and related research and development. Although context may differ between India and

Poland, the latter has set some good examples in water management, which can be useful for India.

Agriculture

The National Mission for Sustainable Agriculture (NMSA) in India has devised strategies to make India's agriculture sector more resilient to climate change. The main objectives of the mission are to identify and develop new varieties of crops and especially climate resistant crops and alternative cropping patterns, capable of withstanding extremes of weather, long dry spells, flooding, and variable moisture availability. The Mission acknowledges that the risks to the Indian agriculture sector due to climatic variabilities and extreme events would be accentuated at multiple levels including at the levels of crop or livestock, farm or cropping system and the food system. Adverse impacts on agricultural production would be severe in the absence of appropriate adaptation and mitigation measures with far reaching consequences in terms of shortages of food articles and rising prices which could endanger the food and livelihood security of our country. The Mission, therefore, seeks to transform Indian agriculture into a climate resilient production system through suitable adaptation and mitigation measures in the domain of crops and animal husbandry. These interventions would be embedded in research and development activities, absorption of improved technology and best practices, creation of physical and financial infrastructure and institutional framework, facilitating access to information and promoting capacity building. The implementation of NMSA up to the end of 12ᵗʰ Five Year Plan would require additional budgetary support of Rs. 1, 08, 000 crore.[30]

Agriculture diversification, climate resilient crops, organic farming etc are recognized as areas of cooperation between India and Poland. Ambassador Mohta also pointed out that agriculture and food processing can be areas of cooperation between India and Poland. Both the countries can share their experiences in the relevant sectors of agriculture. Although Indian agriculture sector is still lagging far behind, it needs technology and capital infusion at a large scale.

Research and Development: Knowledge and Information Sharing

Research and development (R&D), and knowledge and information sharing are key to both mitigation and adaptation process to climate change. They are also essential for technological progress and its applicability. R&D cooperation under the bilateral as well as the EU's Seventh Framework Programme (FP7) can also be promoted for innovation in renewable energy, water and agriculture sectors. Indian researchers and research organizations can participate in joint research programmes as well. India, Poland and EU can develop the synergy between FP7 and India's Mission Strategic Knowledge on climate change. At the bilateral level, India-Poland cooperation in areas of science and technology is also crucial. The Council of Scientific and Industrial Research and the Indian National Science Academy have ongoing scientific exchange programmes with the Polish Academy of Sciences.

Major Challenges

At the policy level, India and Poland have identified energy security as major area of cooperation. At the practical level, a lot of efforts need to be put in place to facilitate energy cooperation. Although shale gas has potential to meet energy demands in India as well as Poland, environmental consequences are yet to be examined. Some scholars have cautioned that shale gas would have severe environmental implications. Scientists fear that 'the process of fracking to extract shale gas could have massive environmental consequences that will cause far more damage than good to the energy sector'.[31] To import coal from Poland, India also needs to improve infrastructural facilities. Since Indian corporations are trying to import more coal from the coal abundant countries, infrastructure needs to be improved.

In the areas of environment, India and Poland have yet to take substantive initiatives to cooperate in water management and environmental protection, etc. As discussed above, India's renewable sector provide huge potential for cooperation between the countries, but there is no crucial steps taken by the government and private sector to harness opportunities. It is pertinent to mention that India and Poland have not encouraged any research project or programme to examine to potential for cooperation in these areas. Research and academic exchange are required to understand the need to society and formulating an appropriate strategy for cooperation. Civil society organizations and business are also not giving due consideration to such issues.

Concluding Remarks

India and Poland have potential for developing a vibrant energy and environment partnership in the framework of New Delhi's NAPCC. Energy and environment cooperation would not only promote sustainable development but also lead to widen their partnership. Production of shale gas provides another opportunity for cooperation. Today India is trying to increase generation of clean and renewable energy and diversify its energy security. If Poland partners in shifting India's growth and economic structure, it will make India-Poland relations more robust, dynamic and sustainable. Energy and environment are intrinsically related to social and economic development, therefore, India-Poland cooperation in these areas would expand horizons of their relationship as well as make it 'people centric'.

Endnotes

1 Planning Commission. "Environment and Climate Change," Eleventh Five Year Plan, p. 191. http://plann ingcommission. nic.in/plans/planrel/ fiveyr/11th/11_v1/11v1_ch9.pdf (Accessed July 26, 2013).

2 Ibid

3 The Planning Commission. *Integrated Energy Policy: Report of the Expert Committee,* 2006, p.54. http://planning commission.gov.in/reports/genrep/ rep_intengy.pdf (Accessed September 1, 2013).

4 Ibid., p. xiii .

5 The Energy and Resources Institute (TERI). "India's Energy Security: New Opportunities for a Sustainable Future," (New Delhi: The Energy and Resources Institute, 2010), p. 5.

6 Ibid., pp. 5-6.

7   Patryk Kugiel and Lidia Puka. "India's Energy Thirst: Opportunities for Poland," The Polish Institute of International Affairs (PISM), Bulletin, No. 68 (521), June 24, 2013.

8   Vikas Dhoot. "Coal-Starved India Inc Importing From Canada," *The Economic Times,* November 29, 2013.

9   Ministry of Coal, Government of India. International Cooperation, http://coal. nic.in/chap60102.pdf (Accessed September 1, 2013).

10 "India, Poland Foster Growing Cooperation," *Warsaw Business Journal*, October   21,   2013,   http://www.wbj.pl/article-64100-india-poland-foster-growing-cooperation.html?typ=wbj (Accessed November 29, 2013).

11 Press Information Bureau. "Steel Minister Visits Poland Strengthens Bilateral Cooperation in Steel Making and Coal Mining," October 29, 2013. http://pib. nic.in/newsite/PrintRelease.aspx?relid=100300   (Accessed November 29, 2013).

12 Ministry of Petroleum and Natural Gas, Government of India. "Shale Gas: Key Considerations for India," 2013, p. 3. http://www.ey.com/Publication/ vwLUAssets/Shale_Gas_-_Key_considerations_   for_   India/$FILE/ EYIN1210-084-Shale-gas.pdf (Accessed November 29, 2013).

13 The Hindustan Times. "India Approves Policy for Shale Gas and Oil Exploration,"   http://www.hindustantimes.com/India-news/NewDelhi/India-approves-policy-for-shale-gas-and-oil-explor   aton/Article1-1126658.aspx (Accessed September 1, 2013).

14 Ministry of Petroleum and Natural Gas. p. 7.

15 Ibid.

16 Ministry of New and Renewable Energy, Government of India. "Jawaharlal Nehru National Solar Mission: Towards Building Solar India," p.1. http:// india.gov.in/allimpfrm s/alldocs/15657.pdf, (Accessed September 10, 2013).

17 Ibid, p. 3.

18 Ibid.

19 Dinoj Kumar Upadhyay. "Expanding EU-India Cooperation in Energy and Environment Sectors," Issue Brief, (New Delhi: Indian Council of World

Affairs, 2012).

20 Ministry of the Environment, Republic of Poland, GreenEva, Winners 2010, 2011 and 2012, Warsaw, 2013. www.greenevo.pl. (Accessed September 11, 2013).

21 Indian Wind Energy Association. http://www.inwea.org/ (Accessed September 10, 2013).

22 Forbes India. "Renew Power: Tapping into India's Wind Energy," Potentialhttp://forbesindia.com/arti cle/hidden-gems/renew-power-tapping-into-indias-wind-energy-potential/36029/1#ixzz2iMDjV6Wg (Accessed September 10, 2013).

23 S.P. Garnaik. "National Mission for Enhanced Energy Efficiency, Bureau of Energy Efficiency, New Delhi," http://moef.nic.in/downloads/others/Mission-SAPCC-NMEEE.pdf (Accessed September 10, 2013).

24 Joshua Chaffin and Pilita Clark. "Poland Vetoes EU Emissions Plan", *Financial Times*, March 9, 2012, http://www.ft.com/cms/s/0/c8665b2c-6a1a-11e1-b54f-00144feabdc0.html#axzz2mJ35h3ub (Accessed November 29, 2013).

25 United Nations Education, Scientific and Cultural Organization. "The World Water Development Report 2009,"p. 3.

26 Ministry of Water Resources, Government of India. "National Water Mission Under National Action Plan on Climate Change," http://india.gov.in/allimpfrms/alldocs/15658.pdf (Accessed September 15, 2013).

27 Zia Haq "India Facing Water Crisis," *The Hindustan Times*, December 8, 2011, New Delhi.

28 Water 2010, organized by Confederation of Indian Industry, New Delhi, cited in Ghosh, Ahona, A Drop in the Ground, *The Economic Times*, 20 December 2011, New Delhi.

29 Zia Haq, 2011.

30 Department of Agriculture and Cooperation, Ministry of Agriculture, Government of India. "National Mission For Sustainable Agriculture Strategies for Meeting the Challenges of Climate Change", 2010, http://agricoop.nicin/Climatechange/ccr/National%20Mission%20For%20Sustainable%20Agriculture DRAFT -Sept-2010.pdf (Accessed September 15, 2013).

31 Sir David King, cited by Ruth Bradshaw. "Fracking Could Have Environmental Consequences", http:// www.uswitch.com/gas-electricity/news/2013/09/17/ fracking-could-have-environmental-consequences/ (Accessed November 29, 2013).

Chapter 9

India-Poland Defence Cooperation

Vijay Sakhuja

Introduction

Defence cooperation is driven by a number of factors such as modernization of the military, self-reliance in defence production, building up the indigenous military industrial capacity, etc. Sometimes, defence cooperation serves politico-diplomatic purposes. In turn these contribute to national security, sovereignty protection and preclude adverse impacts of military sanctions by other external sources.

Defence cooperation with Poland has always been an important part of India's military force structure, its modernization and technological up-gradation. Historically, the Soviet Union was the major arms supplier to India. Poland being part of the larger Soviet military industrial complex was well known for its expertise in some high technology areas, such as armoured recovery vehicles, warship building, optoelectronics and radar systems. Poland's assistance in modernizing and updating the Soviet equipment has been very critical for India's defence sector. Significantly, the payment for the hardware and services were favourable for India.

The period between 1981 and 1988 has been termed as the golden age for Polish-India defence cooperation and India imported US$ 250 million worth of equipment overshadowing other competitors. In the post-Soviet period, the first bilateral Memorandum of Understanding (MoU) on defence cooperation between India and Poland was signed in February 2003. In 2004, the Joint Defence Working Group was established to facilitate dialogue in different areas of defence cooperation. The Defence Working Group made its last visit to Poland in April 2010. Another MoU was signed on February 27, 2012 to continue and deepen the existing cooperation between Polish and Indian defence industry.

It has been noted that Poland is not only interested in selling military equipment to India but is also ready for joint ventures and transfer of technology. In the past, Poland has supplied spares as well as technology for maintaining and upgrading several kinds of equipment such as tank recovery vehicles, spares for specific kinds of Soviet aircraft including up gradation technology and maintenance technology.

As far as the Indian Air Force is concerned, India purchased 50 Iskra ("Spark") aircraft in 1974. These were used as a jet trainer for 29 years and decommissioned in 2004. According to an Indian defence website Bharat Rakshak, "During the course of the Iskra's career with the IAF, they have accumulated over 190,000 hours of flying1500 trainee pilots; 54 Pilot Course batches were trained over the years and the attrition rate had been quite low...[however] the Iskras, while being a reasonable training aircraft and good for armament practice, had some limitations in spinning demonstrations...".

Polish shipyards have built naval platforms for India. For instance, between 1974 and 1976, India acquired four landing ships from the Soviet Union and these were built by the Stocznia Marynarki Wojennej or Naval Shipyard Gdynia. The second batch of four vessels of the same class were ordered directly by the Indian Navy and supplied in 1985-1986 and were commissioned in Gdynia. These vessels were well designed, extremely seaworthy and operationally very efficient. One of the vessels was decommissioned after 33 years of service, 9000 operational hours, and had sailed a distance of 166,000 nautical miles.

India in Polish Strategic Thought

It will be instructive to understand India in Polish strategic thought. In a perceptive article on India-Poland relations titled 'Saying Hello to Old Friend Again!: Analyzing Indo- Poland Contemporary Relations', Aleksandra Jaskólska states that the Polish people should 'stop looking at India through media generated 'stereotypes' and will be able to see real India – a country which still have a lot of problems but is also developing very fast'. Jaskólska makes reference to three popular polish web sites *www. onet.pl*, which had 1920 topics which included the word India; www. *wp.pl*, had 1000 matches; and *www.gazeta.pl*, 2023 matches. These web sites present different images of India which vary from politico-strategic and economics issues, social and cultural issues including music. For instance, India's international relations-12; cooperation with Poland-7; Indian economy-7; relations with US-7; relations with EU-4; space industry-3; and military business-4.

It is evident from above that defence and military cooperation or defence sales between India and Poland have not found much favour among the military professionals and military corporate community on both sides and also among security bloggers and casual net surfers. However, some military hardware companies/vendors, particularly from Poland, have been active in India and have attempted to explore the Indian military market. It will be useful to examine the type of military hardware exported by Poland to international customers: Battle tanks, Armoured Combat Vehicles, Large-calibre artillery systems, Combat aircraft, Attack helicopters, Warships, Missiles and missile launchers and a variety of light weapons including personal arms. This is indeed a very large and varied inventory for sales. Besides, Poland is signatory to a number of multilateral arms control regimes such as the Zangger Committee, Nuclear Suppliers Group, Australia Group, Missile Technology Control Regime and the Wassenaar Arrangement and is a responsible supplier of military hardware.

A Polish report titled "Exports Of Arms and Military Equipment From Poland: Report For 2010" published by the Ministry of Foreign Affairs of the Republic of Poland, provides us some idea of the level of military sales between India and Poland. In a table tilted "Main importers from Poland according to value of licenses 2009", India ranks 6ᵗʰ below US, Malaysia, Canada, Algeria and Indonesia. There were 93 export licenses issued and the value of military exports was 21.6 million Euro. In 2010, India ranked 5ᵗʰ among the importers and the total value of military hardware imported was 22.3 million Euro exhibiting a very marginal increase. The report also notes that "Poland should be concerned about the relatively low position of India, which used to be a leading partner of the Polish arms industry."

Bumar Group

It is useful to discuss a major Polish companies engaged in military sales to India. Bumar is a well established Polish military hardware company and has been engaged in the production of ARVs. Since 1999, India has ordered 556 WZT-3M ARVs to support the Indian Army armoured units equipped with T-90 and T-72 tanks. The WZT-3 is based on the PT-91 chassis, the Polish derivative of the T-72M. In 2012, Bumar signed a deal with BELM Limited to deliver 204 WZT-3M Armoured Recovery Vehicles under a US$275 million. Also, it was agreed that the production will be done primarily in India, by BELM, which has already produced 362 WZT-3 supplied for the Indian Army so far. Poland will supply sub-assemblies, kits and components.

According to Rafal Baniak, the Polish Under Secretary of State, Poland is ready to implement new joint projects dedicated to the Indian Army, and that the "Polish arm industry has made much progress and today our potential is much larger than few years ago. An example is Rosomak, which is regarded by experts as one of the best military transporters". As part of the "Strategy of consolidation and supporting the development of Polish defence industry in 2007-2012", the BUMAR Group acquired the 'PHZ CENZIN Sp. zo.' on December 21, 2009.

Joint Exercise with Marines

In November 2011, a combined Indo-Polish special forces exercise 'pk. Tiger Claw' involving the Polish Special Forces and 21st Indian special forces battalion took place at the Counter Insurgency and Jungle Warfare School (CIJWS) in Mizoram (India). According to an Indian spokesperson, "Polish Special Forces soldiers presented a high combat value, efficiently and professionally performing tasks received under extreme environmental conditions." This offers India and Poland to work together on conter terrorism

India, Poland and NATO

It has been New Delhi's policy to shun bloc politics and has supported non-alignment. At the same time, in the changing international landscape, it has developed strategic partnerships with a record number of nations. In 2011, in an unexpected move, NATO offered to share its ballistic missile defence (BMD) technology with India. The proposal is premised on the belief that there is 'commonality of threats' faced by NATO and India and it is willing to share BMD technology as well as the possibility of 'training together'. Although India is developing its indigenous BMD capability, the NATO offer is attractive. However, New Delhi is yet to take a view on this issue, it will not be averse to the idea of joint development and transfer of technology. Poland is a member of NATO, therefore, it can participate in the project as also support the transfer of advanced technologies to India.

India, Poland and the EU

The 2004 communication on the EU-Indian Strategic Partnership lays the foundation of a robust engagement between India and the EU. The India-EU Strategic Partnership Joint Action Plans (2005 and 2008) offer the framework for dialogue and cooperation in the security domain on thematic and specific issues such as global and regional security threats and challenges.

It is in the above context, India and Poland will have to explore the 2003 European Security Strategy (ESS) reviewed in 2008, European Union Common Security and Defence Policy (CSDP) and the India-EU Strategic Partnership Joint Action Plan to explore vistas for developing bilateral and multilateral defence cooperation that could include issues such as (a) counter-terrorism, (b) organized crime including piracy, (c) counter drug and illegal arms trafficking, (d) cyber-terrorism and (e) non-proliferation of weapons of mass destruction and their delivery systems. Developments in Afghanistan and Somalia are also of interest to both India and Poland.

India and Poland have also constituted a Joint Working Group on Counter-Terrorism (JWG-CT). As Polish counter-terrorism and intelligence capability are well recognised, India would definitely benefit from this cooperation.

India, Poland and the Arctic Council

It is an acknowledged fact that the melting of the Arctic sea-ice is offering both opportunities and challenges which accrue in the form of energy resources, marine living resources and shorter shipping routes across the northern waters.

The first Polish polar base was created in 1957 on Svalbard, and a Polish vessel, the "Oceania" regularly organizes expeditions to Svalbard. Likewise, On July 30, 2007, India established a scientific research station *Himadri* at Ny Alesund. In fact India's engagement in the Arctic dates back to nearly nine decades when it signed the Svalbard Treaty on February 9, 1920 which entered into force on August 14, 1925.

The Arctic Council, established in 1996 is an intergovernmental group of Arctic states which promotes cooperation, coordination and interaction among the Arctic States, on common Arctic issues. The Council has provision for observer status for states and the five permanent observers are: Britain, France, the Netherlands, Poland and Spain. India is interested in obtaining an Observer status in the Arctic Council. Apparently the Indian Prime Minister had proposed mutual consultations on the Arctic during the official visit of the Polish Prime Minister to India and Poland could consider supporting India in the Arctic Council. In October 2010, Poland hosted the Political Sciences Conference on the Arctic at the University of Lublin. Such interactions can help develop common programmes between Poland and India for the Arctic.

Exploring Vistas

India is expected to spend nearly US$ 50 billion for new acquisitions in the next five years and 70 per cent of its military hardware is imported. India wants to diversify its sources to avoid dependence on a few who could under political pressures impose sanctions thereby stalling the military modernisation. India's military acquisition process has undergone significant transformation and the Defence Procurement Policy (DPP) encourages global tenders and provides greater transparency in the competition process. The new guidelines encourage foreign arms manufacturers to develop partnerships with Indian companies both public and private and this could be a good way for Poland to remain a major supplier of military hardware to the Indian establishment. In this context, participation by PZL-130 Orlik produced in Poland in the RFP for the delivery of 75 basic training planes merits attention.

Poland and India defence cooperation cannot be seen as only buyer and seller relations. Both must move towards long term and comprehensive cooperation such as joint research, development and production of weapons system.

In this context, it is important to cite the remarks of Ambassador Monika Kapil Mohta, India's ambassador to Poland in an interview titled "A Cold Country of Warm People" made on December 21, 2011. It was stated that "Our defence relationship is tried and trusted; we have traditional defence ties. Poland has both the capacity and the willingness to deliver to India upgraded defence technologies, which we require in certain areas. So it's a relationship that will certainly have a very bright and very promising future."

Chapter 10

India and Poland's Strategic Perspectives on Afghanistan-Pakistan, Terrorism and Arab Spring

Srikant Paranjpee

Introduction

Changing political dynamics in the Arab world, security and political transition in Afghanistan, evolving security situation in Asia-Pacific and rising non-traditional security threats pose several challenges for both India and Europe including Poland. This chapter focuses on two issue areas; first, it attempts to analyze Indian strategic perspectives in the post Cold War era that have an impact on some of the key regional issues that confront the world today; the Afghanistan-Pakistan situation as it unfolds in the context of the eventual US withdrawal, its connection with terrorism and the implications of the 'Arab Spring', a movement that started with Tunisia and Egypt and appears to spread in other parts of the West Asia in various dimensions; and its impact and the approaches that India has sought to structure to tackle this threat. Second, it aims to locate the points of commonality and diversity in Indian and Polish responses to these challenges.

Strategic Perspectives

India's 'Governing Image' about its strategic thinking is a product of its historical, cultural, geopolitical, socio-economic compulsions; it is a perspective that has grown from a mindset that can best be described as 'civilizational'. During the early years of Independence, India's security policy followed two main trends: one represented India's urge to assert an independent understanding of world affairs in its security policy and second was the assertion of a peace approach to international relations. These principles were reflected in its attempts to build regional solidarity and the spread of regionalism. The early efforts at this included the Asian Relations Conference (1947), the Conference on Indonesia (1949), the Colombo Conference (1954) and the Bandung Conference (1955). However, regionalism has never become a fundamental concern of Asian states. Interstate conflicts caused by unsettled boundaries, existence of large minorities, clash of elites, etc. were some of the serious obstacles. The onset of the Korean War and the resultant Korean system of alliances ended attempts at regional solidarity. The first Afro-Asian conference at Bandung that had sought to expand the approach towards regionalism also was the last such efforts at regionalism. The intrusion of Cold War alliances in Asia slowly eroded the framework of peace approach based on independent understanding. From Bandung onwards there was a slow shift towards the development of a "neutralist" policy that addressed itself to the global concerns of the Cold War conflict. The fundamental tenets of peace and independence were to become the foundations of the new nonaligned policy. The security dimensions of the nonaligned approach were to draw on these basic tenets. They ensured that the strategic doctrine of a country focused on the fundamentals of national interest, as defined by the approaches of peace and independence, and thereby enabled one to structure a security policy to ensure the goals.

Indian security policy during the Nehru era, almost until the India-China war in 1962, rested on his model of development and the policy of defence through development and diplomacy. In essence, this approach accepted the logic of defence through diplomacy and developed a security framework that had its roots in politico-diplomatic activities and the process of modernization through industrial development. Post-1962, India shifted to a 'defence through military preparedness' policy, which was noted in the report of the Ministry of Defence, 1963-64. The Report also observed that the need for a long-term view of defence planning for managing tensions across the border. However, Indian commitment to peace and non-aggression was affirmed.[1]

The late 1960s brought in several changes. At one level, Pakistan sought to reassert itself. Pakistan did this by moving closer to China and also through conflict with India in 1965. By the early 1970s, a new thinking set in. This was the post-Bangladesh era and there was certain degree of credibility about India's position in South Asia. This period saw some serious efforts being made to develop Indian military capability; both consolidation and modernization of the armed forces were undertaken. During the 1970s, Indian policy came to be analysed through the conceptual framework of the regional state system This approach considered India as a regional hegemon, Pakistan as a bargainer or a partner state, small powers of the region as peripheral dependents and extra regional interests as a fourth constituent.

The post-Soviet era of international relations has brought in an entirely new set of conceptual frameworks to the discussion of the regional state system. Changes took place at two levels: the global, relating to transformations in the developed world; and those in the 'Third World'. The global level changes relate to the changes in the approaches to the concept of power, the technological revolutions, especially in the area of Information Technology and the emergence of market economies across the globe. Extra regional intervention for resolving humanitarian crisis situations created by problems of governance or struggle for self determination in the Third World has achieved a new legitimacy in the international forum. Such interventions may come under the umbrella of the United Nations or regional organisations. Cases like Cambodia, Somalia or Yugoslavia, where either the UN or the NATO took an initiative or terrorism related situations like Afghanistan where NATO is operative, or crisis areas in Africa where the African Union takes initiative are now 'acceptable' in international relations. We are presently on the brink of economic and political crisis; two major threats loom: the financial collapse of the western banking infrastructure based on the Breton Woods institutions, and the inability of the UN to deal successfully with series of 'disturbed turbulences' or 'one hundred pinpricks'[2] which have become the hallmark of global war on terror.

The Third World perceptions about these global changes were essentially reactive. On one hand they sought to address the adverse impact of globalization that became visible in the politico-economic and the socio-cultural fields; and the continuing problems of internal security on the other. In case of India, three important developments took place that constitutes a watershed in Indian strategic perspectives of the post Soviet era:

(a) The process of economic liberalization and reform that began under the compulsion of an economically parlous condition in 1991.

The Indian economic reform program led to a sustained average annual growth rate of 8 per cent. India is today giving financial and technical assistance to a large number of developing countries and its food self sufficiency has made it a major interlocutor on issues of food security. Economic diplomacy has now emerged as an important tool in Indian armoury vis a vis both, the developed and the developing world. The focus has now shifted from export promotion to import, investment and services promotion and India's Technical and Economic Cooperation (ITEC) programme has become more diverse both in content and geographical coverage.

(b) The nuclear tests in 1998 and the formal declaration that India was now a nuclear weapons power formally ended the earlier 'deliberate ambiguity' posture of India nuclear policy. Over the years the issue of nuclear and related technologies like space and electronics had come to symbolise the core of the G-8 (Group of industrialized nations) status quoist agenda. The NPT regime with its multifarious dimensions like the Nuclear Suppliers group, Missile Technology Control Regime (MTCR), Fissile Material Cut-off Treaty (FMCT), etc. had sought to place the P-5 (five nuclear weapon powers) in a monopolistic managerial framework. The first symbolic defiance of this restraint came in the form of the 1974 nuclear test at Pokhran. The May 1998 nuclear tests represent this defiant independence at an age where the nuclear regime had become more stringent over the years.

(c) The Indo–US Civilian Nuclear Cooperation Deal that at one level granted India an 'acceptance' in the global nuclear circles and ushered in a more 'realist' perception in India's world view. It is in the backdrop of this nuclear non-proliferation and technology denial regime that one would have to look at the India US nuclear cooperation agreement signed in 2008.[3] The passing of this deal through the International Atomic Energy Agency (IAEA) and the Nuclear Suppliers Group (NSG) and the acceptance by the US Congress symbolizes the success of India to break through the denial regime and gain legitimacy for its stand as a nuclear capable power.

The central debates in India about its strategic perspectives today retain

South Asia centricity as a key feature, assert the need for non intervention in domestic affairs, independent understanding of world affairs and peace approach. Yet, the logic that led India to formulate the nonaligned approach as an alternative world view to the establishment of the cold war does not exist today. The global situation has changed radically. Where does India stand in this? Its traditional revisionist perspective was structured to tackle the status quo created by the great powers. Today, given India's own status, it cannot afford to take a purely revisionist perspective but it needs to participate in the building up of a new order. Indian argument today has centred on the technological and economic capabilities that the country has gained. It is now demanding space in the decision making circles of the world. At one level such a space would enable it to reassert the demands of the Developing World. At another level it may find itself on the same side of the negotiating table along with the countries of the G8. This remains an unresolved dilemma. It is in the context of these positions that one needs to look at the key regional issues of Afghanistan, Pakistan, terrorism and the 'Arab Spring'. It needs to be stressed, however, that these issues are closely interconnected in terms of Indian perspectives; that they are a product of the post Cold War changes that have occurred at a global level.

Terrorism and Afghanistan–Pakistan

Terrorism has been defined as a sub-state application of violence or the threat to use violence with an intention to create panic in the society. It may appear to use guerrilla tactics, but it differs from guerrilla warfare and becomes asymmetric warfare[4] in that terrorists do not hold on to territory like the guerrillas. In terms of contemporary analysis of asymmetric warfare, this kind of a conflict would be witnessed at two levels: Ethnic-separatist terrorism and Post-modern pan-religious terrorism. Ethnic-separatist terrorism revolves around the concept of ethnic nationalism and the right to self-determination. These demands may be articulated by any of the groups in professing ethnic, religious, regional or any other identity. This is a traditional state centric form of terrorism; Post-modern pan-religious terrorism goes beyond the limits of the geopolitical entity of a nation state system. The objectives are abstract and may be defined with reference to the religious resurgence of the post Cold War era.

The 9/11 attacks brought the concept of postmodern terrorism[5] into the forefront. The unfolding of the American response to 9/11 in the form of the Afghan war against Taliban, the eventual spread of terrorism in its modern form in terms of attacks in London, Madrid or Bali; the continuing struggle in Afghanistan, its linkages with Pakistan especially in the context of Osama bin Laden and the enunciation of the Af-Pak policy are all interconnected and continuous issues. The 9/11 attacks were interpreted not as a strike against a nation state (USA) but as a strike against certain value systems that countries like the US had come to adopt. These value systems were based upon norms of representative political systems with liberal socio-economic ideologies. The terrorist groups knew no geopolitical boundaries and carried no national identity. There is likely to be a temptation of projecting this war in the Samuel Huntington's framework of Clash of Civilizations. It needs to be mentioned here that the source was not mainstream religious-civilisational resurgence in general, but the fundamentalist militant groups within the system. For even in its efforts at resurgence, the mainstream religious movements have always remained moderate. Terrorism is not a weapon of religions that have a civilisational base.

There have been two distinct 'western' approaches to counter this new form of terrorism: one the US approach that came to be articulated in the context of the Afghan war against Taliban and the other, the British that was sought to be articulated in the context of the London bombings of 2005. The American approach to counter terrorism was based on two assumptions: that there would be a violent protest/disgust about the attacks on the World Trade Centre and that the world would rally around those who stand against such terrorist tactics that attack innocent civilians. The first of these assumptions has been accepted across the world as valid. The US was able to gain support on humanitarian grounds and support came from diverse sources ranging from the European countries to the Arab world. On the second, there was a hedging of positions and the support was extended 'on principle'; but there was a reluctance to commit human resources to counter terrorist networks. This reluctance was a product of an implicit realization that though the present anti-terrorist posture was targeted against the Islamic Jihadi version of terrorists, the 'Islamic' dimensions of this target were likely to get highlighted.

In a sense, the US, symbolically laid out its 'battlefield'. The central element of this battlefield was the scientific and technological capability to fight a sustained battle against terrorism. The key question would have been how would Osama bin Laden/ Al Qaida counter the US strategy? Al Qaida as symbol of the terrorist groups, in and outside of Afghanistan appear to have had evolved its own alternate strategy to counter the American doctrine. This counter strategy was based on the assumption that they do not have the technological or the military capability to counter strike the US in the battlefield. Thus the counter strategy would have to be based on elements that terrorist organizations can control and rely on. Essentially therefore, they have to evolve their own alternative 'battlefield'. This 'battlefield' would not be based on the use of weapons of war as are universally understood. The use of ideology based on religion appears to be the alternative strategy that is emerging. The battle would now be fought with ideas and propaganda and not weapons of war. Thus the war was fought at two separate levels: one using economics, politics and the military as elements of the battlefield and the other trying to use a propaganda war of ideas and terror as its elements of the alternative battlefield. It was this feature that is most likely to complicate the counter terrorist struggle.

It was precisely, this dimension that was to be picked up by Tony Blair in the post London bombings of 2005. The terrorists of the London bombings were not 'outsiders' as in the case of 9/11, they were British of may be the first or the second generation. The use of force would have severe limitations in this counter terrorism strategy. It is here that the concept of fighting ideas with counter ideas was born. Tony Blair sought to counter the idea of Jihad with an equally powerful idea of nationalism. An idea that had been given a makeover in the post Soviet European order through the creation of several new states on the basis of ethnic nationalism based right to self determination. Blair's attempt to reassert the sense of British nationalism was now to be a new strategy to counter this post modern form of terrorism.

It is in the context of this background that one would have to understand Indian concerns about terrorism, both, at the domestic level and at the international level in the context of Afghanistan–Pakistan and the concerns about the growing threat of a radical influence in the aftermath of the changes on the Middle East.

Indian strategic perceptions about problems of terrorism have two points of focus: one is the Pakistan centric perception that has an inevitable linkage with events in Kashmir and two, the articulation of the problem in the idiom of 'communal tensions' rather than terrorism. Indian strategic perception about terrorism, particularly in Kashmir, has always been Pakistan centric. The presentation of the problem has been structured as an undeclared, low intensity conflict or proxy war that is conducted by Pakistan and is fought through various militant groups. The US has sought to contain the problem within the geopolitical boundaries of South Asia. The Clinton version of Kashmir being the most dangerous place in the world is a product of this containment.

A distinction needs to be made in the two levels of militancy in Kashmir. One level is that of the demands made by the Kashmiri populace within the geopolitical framework of the nation state of India. These demands may be articulated by any of the groups in Kashmir, they would constitute legitimate demands that the State needs to address. The second level of militancy is a product of an abstract ideological struggle that has come to be labeled as 'Jihad'. This level of an agitation does not recognize any geopolitical boundaries and is a global war against the system. This is as much a threat to countries like India as it would be to Pakistan. It is at this second level threat that the counter terrorist strategy needs to be addressed.

The 9/11 events have provided a breakthrough in global perceptions that India needs to exploit. One India needs to articulate its problems in Kashmir in the conceptual paradigm of terrorism. Two, follow-up this linkage with a public statement of its willingness to use forces against those agencies that foster this terrorism. Implicit in this statement would be the element of hot pursuit. However, political and military compulsions may limit this option. Traditionally, India has always articulated a non-military strategy for the resolution of border disputes. The use of diplomacy and consideration of force as a last option have been the twin basis of Indian strategy. India is well aware of the resultant political uncertainties of a cross border military action. The determination of staying within the boundaries of the Line of Control during the Kargil conflict symbolizes this resolve. The military capabilities required to initiate, conduct, sustain and pursue such a cross border action against Pakistan are of a very high order. Any such action would require an overwhelming military superiority. In the case of Pakistan, any such action that is long drawn would certainly be counterproductive. Long drawn actions provide for time to the enemy to regroup and redraw on one's resources. And as Afghanistan is now showing, the battle lines tend to get blurred.

Over the years, the pan-Islamic militant organizations have

succeeded in making inroads into the Pakistani political system. The Mujahedeen of the 1980s who fought the Soviets with American aid have now been transformed into a pan-Islamic force that calls for 'Jihad'. They also appear to have proliferated into several groups. Pakistan has been accused of aiding the growth of such militant movements as those who have operated in Chechnya, and other areas in the former Soviet Republics of Central Asia. The Pakistani connection with the Taliban is well-known. It is not that the political system is itself in the control of these outfits. But, there appears to exist an uneasy coexistence between the ruling elite and these militant organizations. Given their extra territorial linkages and operations they emerge as autonomous operators in the system. It is in this context that India looks at America's Af-Pak strategy and its long term implications to the region of South Asia.

The US President declared the Af-Pak policy-I on March 27, 2009 and the Af-Pak policy-II on December 2, 2009 with a new strategy and boldness to wipe out terrorism which goes by the expression: 'surge and exit'.[6] President Obama acknowledged the linkage between Afghanistan and Pakistan in terms of Pakistan being a safe haven for the al Qaeda groups. In mid-May 2012, at a NATO summit meeting held in Chicago, President Obama and leaders of America's NATO allies formally agreed to hand over the primary role in providing security in Afghanistan to the Afghans themselves in the summer of 2013, beginning the end of the US involvement in a decade-long war.[7]

Indian concerns about the American policy in the Afghanistan–Pakistan region and the issue of terrorism can be summarised as follows:

(a) Indian interests in Afghanistan have taken a concrete shape with the signing of the strategic partnership agreement on October 4, 2011. The agreement indicated a movement beyond the earlier Indian policy towards Afghanistan of providing non–military help in the form of development and reconstruction aid. India decided to expand the training of Afghan National Security Forces (ANSF), particularly the Afghan National Police (ANP), so as to build local capacity for providing security. The trade and economic agreements were a reiteration of India's commitment to Afghanistan's economic growth, and its role as a "bridge" between South Asia and Central Asia. India has also emphasised on "regional economic cooperation" indicating India's vision of binding the countries in the region through a mutually beneficial cooperative framework.[8]

(b) Indian concern regarding the American policy focuses on two issues: its continuing soft approach towards Pakistan and its inclination for conducting a dialogue with the Taliban. The former is seen despite the Pakistani policy towards al Qaeda, the Haqqani network and Osama bin Laden and the American awareness of this linkage. The American State Department has now blacklisted the Haqqani network.[9]

Arab Spring

The West Asian countries face a peculiar problem that Pakistan shares. Traditionally, there has been a state on 'uneasy coexistence' between the ruling elite and the more radical Islamic groups in their countries. The problem becomes more complex when these groups forge links with pan Islamic militant (terrorist) organizations. The threat to the political stability of the political regimes from any agitation sponsored by the militant groups has always been real. These states have therefore always done a tight rope walking on issues of terrorism. It is this that has been a matter of concern in the context of the outcome of the 'Arab Spring'.

India viewed the 'Jasmine Revolution' in Tunisia as a spontaneous and wide-spread democratic movement.[10] The ouster of President Ben Ali in January 2011 brought to an end the single-party rule of the RCD Party, the transformation of the Tunisian political system into a multi-party democracy was largely peaceful and non-violent. Following the National Constituent Assembly elections, a new government was sworn in toward the end of 2011 and the task of drafting a new Constitution began. The Egyptian President Hosni Mubarak was ousted and the army took command over the Egyptian political system in January 2011. Elections followed and the Islamist president from the Egyptian Muslim Brotherhood Mohammed Morsi proved victorious. The tussle between the elected government and the armed forces continued with the army deciding to dissolve the Parliament. The so called Arab Spring that began with Tunisia did not follow the Tunisian pattern of a transition to civilian government. Foreign intervention in Libya by the NATO brought in chaos, Syria continues to be engulfed in a civil war, Yemen has seen cosmetic change, and protest continues to be brutally put down in Bahrain and Saudi Arabia and in the

Afghanistan–Pakistan region American intervention continues to remain a problem.

The 'Arab Spring' needs to be looked at more as an 'Arab Awakening' rather than a pro democracy movement that the 'Arab Spring' as a term seems to imply. The Middle East political system has traditionally rested on a certain political equation between the political elite and the populace. This equation may be looked as the role of the ruling class in terms of providing the necessary amenities to the populace that would include the fundamental requirements for living like food, shelter and clothing with a welfare factor to take care of. The populace in these states would not be living is abject poverty but would be on the margins of a good life. The corresponding obligation on part of the populace appears to be that they do not question the ruling class and the political system that they have evolved; be it monarchical, authoritarian, military or any other. These political systems did not permit any political dissent or demonstrations, for more than half a century since the people have been kept down.

The last decade saw the knowledge revolution take shape and spread throughout the world. It spread through the technological revolution ushered in by the explosion in information technology, especially through the Third World. With a massive amount of knowledge freely available to the youth, the Arab youth realised what they had missed. The revolution seemed to bypass the entire West Asia leaving the youth in a time warp of the earlier life style. The other aspect that was seen was that those who were within the ruling elite community did get the benefit of this revolution, the bulk of the populace appeared to be kept at bay. It was this that eventually exploded in the form of the agitation that made the youth to come to the streets. It was spontaneous and it was justified. However, over time, as the agitation spread both in its intensity and the geographic area, it was those in the opposition to the then governments that were well organised who took control of the movement. In most cases these were the Muslim Brotherhood. It is precisely this factor that has become a matter of concern in the Middle East. It may be interesting to note that while the monarchies of the Middle east appear to have retained the stability of their political system, it is countries like Tunisia, Egypt, Libya, Syria that have seen the impact of popular uprising. These countries do have their individual dimensions. In Syria it is a conflict against the minority Alawites who are the ruling class, in Bahrain it is a Shia uprising against the Sunni rule. In Egypt, the army is keen on keeping control while in

Turkey the government is trying to retain the secular identity of the country. It would only be some time before the monarchies face the wave of the knowledge revolution and the awakening that has spread due to the modern technology. While the populace that has fought the earlier authoritarian regime may not look for a switch from the earlier system to an Islamic one under the Muslim Brotherhood, the fact remains that the 'secular' opposition remains fragmented across the West Asia. In essence, one may see a long winding social churning of the Arab societies, at times bloody at times not so peaceful, that would eventually change the political ethos of the region. In all of this change, India appears to wait and not take sides. It was only in Tunisia that the government response was relatively fast; in Egypt India appeared to wait until the change over took place; and in Libya and Syria the Indian position has also been wait and watch.

India and Poland

Where can one search for locating common areas of Indo-Polish perceptions in the contemporary world order? India had also looked at the changes in Poland in the 1970s and the 1980s with interest. In the seventies it focussed on the manner in which the Helsinki Declaration (1975) unfolded as also the impact of the visit by Pope John Paul–II in 1979. In the eighties it was the rise of the Solidarity Movement and its role in the 1989 upheaval. The peaceful transition that Poland effected in the European changes of 1989 and the movement of Poland from a country under the Soviet influence to one that sought to take an independent posture in world affairs was also of interest to India. Eventually Poland joined the NATO in 1999, and played an active role in Iraq and Afghanistan.

Indian perception of Poland is at two levels: One at the bilateral level and the other as a member of the EU and NATO. While in real terms the bilateral level perception tends to override the regional linkages, the Polish identity with Europe and NATO remains a reality. It is the bilateral linkages in the areas of security, political economy, and governance that need to be explained by the two countries. Polish economy was remarkably stable at the time of the US recession and has continued to remain stable in the current European crisis despite the fact that Poland is a member of the EU. This is an advantage in the building up of trade linkages at the bilateral level. At the level of governance, the Indian civil society carries a great deal of empathy for the manner in which Poland sought to evolve a liberal democratic structure in the post 1989 years. Both countries share values of peace, liberty, democracy, rule of law, etc that can operate as a form of normative power in the context of promoting good governance. A case is sometimes made for a strategic partnership between the two countries.[11] Such a partnership would have to focus on both material and non–material elements. The former would include the arrangements that are made to exchange goods and services, which in security area would involve military hardware and technology. This is the political element of the partnership. This concept provides flexibility in the security architecture of the post Cold War era that the earlier formal alliances had denied. It gives either party the ability to manoeuvre its national interest in the anarchic world order along the road map that it has charted for itself and if need be alter or revise it mid course.

Endnotes

1   Ministry of Defence, Government of India. *Annual Report, 1963-64*, p.2.

2   Comment made by Gen. Scowcroft at the discussion hosted by the Centre for National Policy, USA, December 17, 2008.

3   The Civilian Nuclear Cooperation Agreement between US and India was signed in 2008.

4   Therese Delpeach, 'The Imbalance of Terror', *Washington Quarterly* Vol. 25 (1), Winter, 2002, pp. 31-32.

5   This term is borrowed from Walter Laquer "Post Modern Terrorism", *Foreign Affairs,* September/October, 1996.

6   Mainstream, Vol. XLVIII, No 14, March 27, 2010.

7   The New York Times, May 21, 2012.

8   Ministry of External Affairs, Government of India, Text of Agreement on Strategic Partnership between the Republic of India and the Islamic Republic of Afghanistan, October 4, 2011 http://www.meagov.in/mystart php?id=530518343 (Accessed September 18, 2012).

9   Declan Walsh and Eric Schmitt 'U.S. Blacklists Militant Haqqani Network',

The New York Times, September 7, 2012.http://www.nytimes.com/2012/09/08/world/asia/state-department-blacklists-militant-haqqani network.html?_r =0 (Accessed September 18, 2012).

10 Ministry of External Affairs, Government of India. 'Bilateral India-Tunisia Relations,' http://meaindia.nic.in/ mystart.php?id=2001&pg=t (Accessed September 5, 2012).

11 Shrikant Paranjpe, 'India and Russia: The Litmus Test of Strategic Partnership', in P.L. Dash (ed), *India-Russia Relations: The Post Cold War Era*,(Mumbai: Nehru Centre, 2011), pp. 59–60.

Index

www.ingramcontent.com/pod-product-compliance
Lightning Source LLC
Chambersburg PA
CBHW070920270326
41927CB00011B/2647